THE
MORAL
STATE
OF
BLACK
AMERICA

Rodrick Burton

The Moral State of Black America by Rodrick Burton.

ISBN: 0-9754332-6-1

Published by: Advantage Books
www.advbooks.com

Library of Congress Control Number: 2004116582

First Printing: April 2004

04 05 06 07 08 09 10   8 7 6 5 4 3 2 1

Printed in the United States of America

FOREWORD

The initial timetable to complete this book was post seminary, and perhaps even after a period of pastoral experience. Yet at the urging of the Holy Spirit, I was compelled to set aside my plans and accelerate the project. The message within these pages is infinitely more important than personal plans to generate credibility. The fact that this book was published and distributed is solely a testament of the efficacy of God's providence and another example of His longsuffering mercy and patience. To God be the glory!

Rodrick Burton

Table of Contents

Rodrick Burton

INTRODUCTION

In the November 2003 issue of *Ebony*, there was an article addressing marriage and Black Americans entitled, "The Shocking State of Black Marriage." The article stated that in 1963 about 70% of Black families were headed by married couples, but that by 2002 the number was down to 48%.[1] For those who claim to be Christians (and 80% of Black Americans do), this has catastrophic theological implications.

We must remember that God's first ordination was that of marriage, the center of the family (Genesis 24). The statistical representation of the decline in marriage has translated into a general moral decline within Black culture. This is readily apparent from secular empirical studies to five minutes of channel surfing. Something is amiss—with us...within us.

The country is experiencing a collective moral decline, but what about us? Even a cursory glance taken at recent national headlines now bears evidence of troubling signs. Incidents and behavior uncharacteristic of Black America abound. Immediately, many would argue that anecdotal evidence is not an accurate gauge of trends. Others would question whether we blacks can trust the media to present anything more than thinly veiled stereotypical presentations. While this was certainly the case thirty years ago, this argument is arduous to maintain as newsrooms and media organizations across the nation pursue diversity to exhibit professionalism, and most importantly, to attract as many ethnic markets as possible. Again we must ask, what's going on?

February 11, 2003 - The Fox network's immensely popular *American Idol* national television competition eliminated semi-finalist 24 year-old Frenchie Davis after discovering she had recently been employed in the pornography industry. For those who are familiar with Fox broadcasting content, the action was unusual. [2]

March 22, 2003 - An African-American paratrooper attacked fellow soldiers with a hand grenade during the opening days of Operation Iraqi Freedom.[3] Black Muslims hailed Sgt. Hasan Akbar's attack as the revolutionary actions of a new Nat Turner. [4]

May 15, 2003 - Eighteen illegal immigrants died locked in a trailer as trucker Tyrone Williams attempted to smuggle them into the United States. Williams faces a litany of charges relating to the deaths. [5]

June 8, 2003 - One year after his suicide in custody, St. Louis police are still trying to piece together the crimes of Maury Travis, whom many experts believe to be the most prolific Black serial killer in American history.[6]

June 22, 2003 - Authorities in Louisiana are now questioning their race-based assumptions regarding the profiling of serial killers after the capture of Derrick Todd Lee (accused of six murders in Louisiana). Lee was arrested at a Holiday Inn in Atlanta where he was hosting a Bible study.[7]

June 27, 2003 - Chante Jawan Mallard, a 27 year-old nurse's aide, was convicted of murder for hitting a homeless man while returning from a night club and leaving him embedded in her windshield to die as she turned in for the night.[8]

September 10, 2003 - Jayson Blair, former reporter for the New York Times who was fired for plagiarism and fabrication, unrepentantly hailed the signing of a six-figure book deal about his infamous career.[9]

October 1, 2003 - A two-year old toddler was left home alone in Jacksonville, Florida for three weeks as the mother was arrested and put in jail. The mother neglected to let the father, her family, or authorities know that her child was unattended at home. The little girl survived on ketchup and dried pasta.[10]

October 5, 2003 - A woman murdered her mother and the pastor at Turner Monumental AME Church, and then committed suicide just before Sunday morning service.[11]

October 7, 2003 - Two sisters left their six young children at home alone to go to a local Yazoo City, Mississippi nightclub. Five of the six are burned alive as the home caught fire and was destroyed.[12]

October 8, 2003 - In St. Louis Missouri, a 19 year-old mother dashed her infant baby against a curb following a dispute with the child's father.[13]

October 20, 2003 - Opening statements commenced in the trial of John Allen Muhammad, the senior member of the Washington, D.C. sniper duo that terrorized the Washington area randomly killing ten persons while ultimately failing to extort $10 million dollars from the government in 2002.[14]

October 29, 2003 - New Jersey's Division of Family Services is reverberated from a case in which foster parents Raymond and Vanessa Jackson starved four adopted boys. Their six other children were reported well fed.[15]

In my hometown of St. Louis Missouri, the community is catching its breath after a summer that mimicked the video game *Grand Theft Auto*. In the game the player is a car thief who, in addition to stealing cars, must battle rival gangsters and dodge the police. In St. Louis, life not only imitated the game, but transcended it as a quartet of youth embarked on a "crime for thrills" spree that matched the insanity of the original youth perpetrated thrill killings of the late 1950s.[16] Even our nation's capitol, Washington, D.C., is still reeling from a summer of Black violence and gang war on the streets.[17] Some readers may be put off by this recitation of the spectacular, but I would be remiss to report that the empirical data in this book reflects a widespread epidemic of lawlessness and rampant immorality. Marvin Gaye said it best, "makes me want to holler," and we should be collectively hollering in mourning and repentance to our God for this abysmal condition.

Our population stands at 36 million and data shows that 80% of Black Americans claim religious affiliation that is overwhelmingly Christian.[18] Yet, as we pridefully declare our piety and devotion to Jesus Christ, statistics show that we are the robbery kings and queens of America. We are, hands down, the undisputed leaders in internal and external murder. Although we are not the epitome of immorality, today in 2003, we are light years away from our moral state of say, 1963. In those days we had no one but the Lord to look to for deliverance from oppression. A God of justice heard our pleas and collectively exalted us rapidly—more rapidly than any other oppressed people group, to a more equal footing within this society. It was our

11

clergy that pointed out the hypocrisy of American Christianity during the centuries of suffering and exhorted the black masses to pursue biblical holiness individually and collectively. The faith in a God who delivered the Israelites out the hands of numerous powerful oppressors was called upon for our people. As usual, God delivered.

We have been free on paper since the 1964 Civil Rights Act. Our collective buying power is 300 billion dollars[19] and we have been in the inner circles of American power for the last three presidential administrations. While the gap still exists between what Blacks and Whites earn, they have diminished dramatically—things have certainly changed. Unfortunately, as John McWhorter pointed out in *Losing the Race*, the cult of victimology has transfixed our collective psyche.[20] It is from within this cult that the ideological fallacy is maintained that we are better than they. This prideful notion is at the heart of our moral delinquency. It has been subconsciously reasoned that as historical victims of adjudicated lawlessness we now have been licensed to sin.

Despite a rich history of Christian pastoral leadership, this theologically flawed worldview has intoxicated the Black American's worldview and has been unchallenged from the pulpit. The peculiar institution of slavery, the Holocaust, Cambodia's Killing Field, the Intifada and countless other historical tragedies are all part of the continuing cycle of sin unleashed upon the earth by the "fall." The belief that Black victimology makes us more righteous should beg us

12

to question how to measure up compared to the Kurds, the Armenians, the Tibetans, or the Kosovar Muslims. For Christians, the only avenue to individual and collective righteousness is through the blood of Jesus and his church, a gift from God, the Father, for his deserving work.

So when there is no perceivable difference between the cultural actions of those claiming His name and those who do not, there exists a moral emergency. This book is targeted to the Black Christian Clergy as a wake-up call to the fact that the moral state of America is a stench overpowering Christ's message from a people who have a uniquely powerful testimony to America and to the world. Pride did not save us, but it is now pride that prevents a unified call from all pulpits denouncing the landslide of postmodern culture and its secular humanistic worldview. Instead of challenging the mindset of a race to rally material resources historically denied to us, clergy have joined in the race, and in some quarters lead the cry for more!

In all of this, the one responsible for our freedom is overlooked. Our service to Him has been replaced by the profitable world-renowned American materialism idolatry. As we live out this freedom, His message is diluted and insulted by the lives and actions of those whose service to Him means coming to get their "shout on" Sunday morning, then stopping at the liquor store, casino, mall or babies' daddy's house for sex on the way home. Just like the unsaved, we revel in the cult of celebrity to an extent that even our pastors and worship leaders must be exalted. We have our own awards show for gospel music, the Stellar Awards, which is a replication of mainstream productions. We have become contextualized to irrelevancy, our religion being just another quirky characteristic ascribed to our people group. How can we declare the power and supremacy of Christ and Christian living when at the most basic anthropological level, the family, we are in disarray? Paul's scriptural instructions for husbands and wives have been rejected in favor of fictionalized relationships portrayed on *The Young and the Restless* and in Zhane's novels. Since the Sexual Revolution and postmodern culture has declared chastity and biblical sexual mores unrealistic, we have accepted these assumptions rooted in human fallen nature as fact and have joined in this cultural orgy.

We have strayed, impugning Christ's name—and our descent towards de-civilization and rapid demise by our own hands have affirmed it. In writing this book as a seminary student, I was inclined to model after other authors who pick a key passage and exegete their way to their grand point. In an effort to "keep it real," this book shall not take that course; rather it will analyze America, our subculture, and present the reader with the obvious. As we consider Jesus' words, "If anyone loves me, he will obey my teaching," and "He who does not love me will not obey my teaching" (John 14:23a, 24a), no intensive exegesis is necessary to make this point: we do not love Christ because we are not obeying Him. It is apparent that those claiming Christ are not in union with Him, and this is a dangerous condition in which to be. God has promised to oppose those who oppose His Son in whom all things have been given.

Anyone who has serviced in the military is familiar with the oath sworn upon completing the enlistment process. The enlistee swears to defend the country from all enemies foreign and domestic. Similarly, God's words are clear that He will defend His Son's name and strike out in righteous vengeance against all enemies within and without His Kingdom. Furthermore, the blackest darkness is reserved for the unsaved domestic enemies (2 Peter: 17) and for God's corrective discipline is meted for all others within the Kingdom. Do we expect God to sit back as we make light of the work of Christ and His magnanimous grace as we rival the unsaved in debauchery and not expect His discipline? Since the traditional doctrine of Hell has been dumped in modern times for the all-good, feel good version of the gospel, we have lost sight of what Christ has saved us from.

Jesus is waiting for our return to Him. He will lead us to worship the Father in spirit and in truth. The truth is, we have drifted astray. The way back is on our faces in repentance. Our community can be restored spiritually and naturally through an unhindered work of the powerful Holy Spirit. We must remove the stumbling blocks that inhibit our calling others to the faith and our growth within the Kingdom. May the reader be moved to heed the call to show the world yet another great work by Christ Jesus, as intractable problems get solved and many who doubted the power will find it irresistible. We can only look upward for our salvation now, tomorrow and forevermore.

Chapter 1

HOW DID WE GET HERE?

If you hold to my teaching, you are really my disciples. Then you will know the truth, and the truth will set you free. –John 8:31-32

Most people, in fact, will not take trouble in finding out the truth, but are much more inclined to accept the first story they hear. –Thucydides 400 B.C.

In order to gain greater understanding about the present, we must return to America's Pre-Columbus past in order to identify God's purpose for this continent. Prior to Columbus, North America and its inhabitants were ignorant of the Gospel as it had not yet reached these shores. Yet, God's providential grace would see to it that the message would reach them and therein lay the first test of American Christianity. America started out as a European business venture. Columbus, a "Christian," did not sell this expedition to Queen Isabella as a long term missions trip. Moreover, from his own diary he set the tone for the relationship between Europeans and Native Americans. [1]

17

Thus, the first test of American Christianity failed and we shall discuss the nature of our Christianity later. While Columbus is not alone in this precedent, tragically, the Gospel's message would be used as a tool of oppression and submission to the authority of men for hundreds of years thereafter.

Popular American mythology largely focuses on the Puritan escape from religious persecution as opposed to a collage of business ventures by the French, Spanish and English. Despite centuries of exegetical study and a litany of learned church fathers, the European mind was unchallenged as to the concept of universal human equality under God. This Satanic stratagem of racial pride and superiority has long served his campaign to taint the witness of Christ worldwide. This fact is hard to swallow but historically correct. Tragically, even as the colonies would introduce African slave labor, opposition arose to the idea of converting the Blacks. The Puritan forefathers were more vigorous in their pursuit of earthly riches than those promised by Christ (Matt. 6:19). Justo Gonzalez, a Christian historian, noted that "in 1667 a law was passed declaring that baptism did not change a slave's condition"—another indication of the degree to which established religion was willing to bend to the interest of the powerful. [2] So we see that from colonial days that the Gospel was tragically mutated to serve the idol of the market- place; moreover, despite man's stumbling blocks, God would see that the Gospel would be disseminated through the Great Awakenings I and II. Yet, as slavery existed (through its practices of breeding, brutality, and family dissection throughout the English colonies) a philosophical construct was adopted to soothe troubled spirits. The wonderful truth preached by Jonathan Edwards, George Whitfield and others calling on one to have a personal relationship with God through Christ on an individual level emancipated a collective blame for corporate injustice. This same belief is widespread among White Christians and was well documented in the award winning book *Divided By Faith*. [3] This individualized separation between real life and the spiritual state blended into the American identity as we gained our independence.

Separation of church and state is one of the most loudly heralded attributes of our nation. Curiously, American Christianity has always laid claim to this land being Christendom. That claim which was again boisterously levied the summer of 2003 as an Alabama supreme court judge refused to move a Ten Commandments monument from a public courthouse, as well as a *USA Today* survey showing an unwillingness to allow an Islamic monument (or Buddhist, or Hindu) equal footing, highlights the bipolarity in our thinking. [4] On the one hand we declare the separation to be the best way to govern, and on the other, we declare that our founding fathers (many Enlightenment influenced Deists) formed a Christian nation. American Christianity has always pointed to the Godly (never Christ)

19

acknowledgment adorning courts, money, and the Constitution as evidence of national Christian identity. We must not overlook the numerous historical instances when violent means were used to deal with heretics (Mormons), Jews, and even Catholics as they attempted to exercise their constitutional right of freedom of religion. American Christianity is amnesic of such episodes as most Americans are about bad history. This brings us to the ultimate question for practitioners of American Christianity: who comes first, Christ or America?

Regarding America, again we must ask, how did we get here? Why did the United States come into existence? This question has been answered from a standard historical perspective; a mythological patriotic perspective; a critical historical perspective; and even an Afrocentric perspective; but has it been answered in a critical historical Christian perspective? I will attempt to do that here because it is imperative that Americans who claim to be Christians put down the blinders of individualism and aim to understand the big picture: the expansion of what Luther termed the "invisible church." No one will dispute that in terms of human history, America has been and is the most profitable experiment in civilization. Conversely, in the context of Christian history, it has been the site of five catastrophic failures. Before we go further, I must insert this disclaimer. Obviously, God's providential grace has been at work in American history and only He knows the scores of souls harvested into the kingdom by the Gospel message. The five failures are in no way attributable to our Father but to the deeds and misdeeds of men who have declared themselves Christians.

The first failure of American Christianity was the Columbus precedent. North and South America were teeming with unreached peoples struggling in a variety of ways to learn the Great Spirit's will. God created these indigenous people spiritually sensitive and desired they be brought into his truthful knowledge. Columbus then entered the scene on a mercantile expedition, and from his own log we can read as the thinly veiled enthusiasm to convert the natives eroded into a lascivious thirst for plunder. [5] Follow-up expeditions by the Jesuits were little more than exercises in psychological warfare and pre-colonial reconnaissance. The monetary focus of the Europeans superceded all other concerns, and thereby set forth a consistent and bloody communion between the Native Americans and Neo-Americans. There have been a minute number of souls who developed a concern to properly contextualize the gospel to the exploited, marginalized, and violently defeated original stewards of the land. The failure to present the gospel in love to the Native Americans, as opposed to a means to an end, was the first mistake of American Christianity.

American Christianity initially stood silent as a new mutation of an ancient sin came to birth. Slavery has been around as long as man and it is interesting that it was the Muslims who really turned the Europeans on to tapping Africa for their burgeoning slave trade. Surprisingly, many of the persistent stereotypes and attitudes about Blacks were adopted by Europeans in close observation of veteran Muslim slave traders. It is remarkable irony that historical Muslim involvement in the African slave trade is unacknowledged to the extent that Islam is considered a worthy alternative for African-Americans due to its perceived clean hands regarding slavery. [6]

The American slave trade (north, central and south) did something unusual in human history by creating new people groups. In our case it was the Black Americans. The process was simple. Like any competent farmer, the best candidates were picked and transferred from Africa to America. Transported in abominable conditions, the voyage induced a survival of the fittest where those who survived were sold at auction.

At the plantation, with profits beckoning, cattle breeding science was applied to human chattel. Female slaves were forced to breed with the strongest and most virile males. Simultaneously from day one, a sweeping social re-engineering went into effect as the African, injected into a new social paradigm, was forced to sever all connections to past family, tribe and traditions. Only the new language was permitted as the sole means of communication. As all aspects of life were unstable, the slaves introduction to a new religion, most commonly used as a necessary means of control, was embraced by the slave as an unshakable given. That which was meant for bad was used for good and God's glory, and through those oppressed souls God would judge the nation.

The Lord saw to it that the good news of the Gospel spread through the land with two Great Awakenings. As many declared it a Christian nation, the actions that bore out through the implementation of Manifest Destiny proved otherwise. Yet from early on pastors would play a pivotal role in the success of this experimental state. Clergy would declare our existence and actions the will of God while thumbing our noses at the Old World, heralding the resolute separation between church and state. In the meantime, the Old Testament, Darwinism, groupthink and every psychological mechanism were employed to justify the barbarity of our peculiar institution. So effective was this legacy of denial, it still persists through collective amnesia and silence ongoing until this day! Next we must consider the blood-soaked watershed in American History: The War between the States.

The Civil War was not fought over singular lofty states rights' aspirations; It was waged against a consortium of pre-fascist states intent on retaining repression and human exploitation as a valid lifestyle. The Civil War not only was the tragic outcome of the maintenance of an immoral cultural regime, but the end of the American feudal era. The industrial age would expand exponentially due to the war and in its wake dispensing freedom to the slaves as America poised to enter a new era.

Many today would be astounded by the tenor and variety of civil rights that were pursued vigorously during Reconstruction. Twentieth Century civil rights veterans would be bewildered by the efforts of Whites working to integrate Blacks as equal participants in American society while being met with violent resistance. An unrepentant South used terrorist tactics to derail the reconstruction process. Their final success was ideological, admitting no wrong but appealing to a base view of racial unity in keeping blacks socially subordinated. Despite ranks of seminary trained preachers, few were able or brave enough to declare the truth about race. God settled the race question in the New Testament. Our one world composed of many nations is viewed in two delineations by God: the saved and unsaved. Today we have the luxury of genetic scientists declaring the illusionary and human created racial construct as bogus, affirming God's position on the subject years ago. However, the longtime rejection of God's truth about racial equality was the foundation for mistake number two: American Christianity's support of slavery.

In the years following Reconstruction's failure, the South executed a propaganda coup de grace that persists into this era. They recharacterized their bloody rebellion as nothing more than a bid for the continuance of a noble lifestyle, admittedly class and race conscious, but nothing more. The heritage of dissent was framed as noble and honorable as any gentlemen's disagreement. Tragically, the Black victims of that age would bear the brunt of what psychiatrists call "transference." The South's anger and shame for defeat was dumped upon the powerless. As the North faced mass immigration by Europeans, they followed the South's lead in accepting a social discourse that erected racial barriers. European immigrants would find that the fastest and easiest track to American solidarity was found in the mutual hatred of the Negro.

With nowhere to hide, Blacks bore out the nadir of race relations in the bosom of Jesus as their fleshly bodies were extracted for lynching. Despite the depths of sin exhibited by a Christian nation, God's mercy shown brightly on Los Angeles' Azuza Street. Sadly, even there as racial unity existed in the heart of the revival, the wicked reality of two Americas was reinstated at its conclusion. The years following the 1906 revival are some of the darkest in American history. We suffered economic collapse during the Great Depression and two world wars. American Christianity's failure to address the racial oppression and oppose the codification of discrimination in the years following the Civil War was mistake number three.

The Civil Rights victory of the 1960's still astonishes the world. Humanism and pride rarely credit the fact that the movement for equality and social justice was led by a Christian organization and headed by a Christian clergyman, Martin Luther King, Jr. The non-violent response to violent opposition played worldwide over a fledgling international medium: Television. As the Western world, headed by America, faced off against godless communist Russia, television exposed its hypocrisy to the world. American Christianity issued no apologies and formally allied itself with the conservative political camp. It adopted the view that anyone criticizing American was squarely aligned with our enemies. Martin Luther King, Jr. was declared a commie and his followers like minded agitators. Instead of thankfulness that a Black Intifada didn't erupt on these shores, the grievances of the oppressed were ignored and American Christianity solidified its racial division within Christ's church.

Unexpectedly, a further tragedy ensued as the youthful Baby-Boomers rejected the faith of their fathers who were modeling a conditional Christianity and initiated an era of collective and societal disorder. Heretical religions gained a foothold as young Boomers searched elsewhere for the truth they didn't see in American Christianity. Secular humanism gained prestige as it declared the crimes of the past wrong, championed racial equality, and committedly called for historical accuracy in liberal political quarters. Ostracized and rejected for ages by mainstream Christianity, the Black Church married a liberal bride unaware of the long term effects of such a union.

Despite the dramatic changes to America in a Postmodern age, American Christianity is still divided by faith. Each faith camp remains embedded in secular political ideologies. The Right remains wrong for its mythological view of history, its unrepentance and Pharisean morality; the Left wrong for its rejection of moral absolutes, its hedonism, and universalism. Neither Black nor White Christians should be beholden to either camp. The response to the Civil Rights Movement was failure number four for American Christianity.

September 11, 2001, was the latest and fifth failure of American Christianity. In the wake of an attack by religious zealots, American Christianity pronounced where its faith rested to a world magnetically focused upon it. That faith is not dependant on the Savior's protective gaze, even though all things have been given to Him. No, American Christianity's trust lies within the power its bombs. It has led the charge to close ranks and has rejected reaching outward. American Christianity took a leading role in throwing a national pity party. It was silent as voices called for the use of torture as a legitimate means to gain information to stave off further attacks. [7] American Christianity declared us pure victims while denying any depravity in our foreign policies. It declared and confirmed the hierarchy of humanity, ours worth more than theirs. American Christianity believes that the Gospel is best shared from a position of numerological and technological strength. Fortunately for America, our God is patient and longsuffering. How many more chances will He allow American Christianity to fail –we don't know. We do know that He desires American Christianity to become Christ like. He desires our allegiance first and foremost to His Son. He desires us to worship in spirit, truth and unity. That day has not yet dawned in America and perhaps it may not come until He comes. Until that time we must strive to be obedient to Christ and His word as Christians in America.

The Black Church's union with liberalism has wreaked havoc within our churches and within our community. This is a call to dissolve that union. Joining the conservative quarter is not the answer. The answer lies in a return to the basic Gospel truth. All the power we need to restore and transform our communities rests in the hands of Jesus.

The Nineteenth Century's clash with theological liberalism was a harbinger of an ongoing religious debate in American Christianity. In recent years mercantile driven multiculturalism and liberalism have continued to cry for truthful history, challenging the idealized American history championed in conservative circles. Liberalism declared fundamental Christianity mythological as well. It is believed that religious fundamentalism cannot coexist with an accurate portrayal of American history. It can. Yet, the unrepentant nature of American Christianity has drawn the liberal assumption.

Currently, Liberalism demands that the Black Church retain and support the role of perpetual victimization. This is morally killing us and stunting our cultural growth. Pastoral voices of dissent are left nowhere but the Right, and this should not be. Postmodernism multiculturalism have eroded the historically fundamentalist Gospel message by demanding philosophical concessions in order to remain allegiant. The power of Jesus Christ has given way to the power of the vote. Religious leaders in the conservative camp may have more liberty to preach the Gospel but must attend to the role as political spoilers and hacks to remain in the Right's good graces. Black conservatives have not challenged American Christianity's Dr. Strangelove doctrine: How I stopped worrying (about world peace) and learned to love the bomb (as long as we have the most). The Black Church must unify and separate from both camps in order to reclaim our collective allegiance to King Jesus. God has saved and, delivered us, brought us honor in the eyes of men. He gave us spiritual and natural freedom. What have we done with it?

Many scholars, sociologists, and citizens at large have declared the social problems intractable. Liberals explain that these problems are complex and rooted in a history of oppression while conservatives declare that they are all lapses of personal responsibility. Both are right. Black Americans can no longer avoid its problems by hiding behind the discourse of blame. God is the only one able to assign unequivocal blame, but He goes further by providing absolution and solutions. How dare we Black Christians obsess over who is to blame? Does God? Let's get real for a moment. For all the talk about accepting responsibility coming out of conservative circles, neither a conservative nor a liberal United States Government has or will be issuing any apologies for slavery in this republic of lawsuits. We must transcend the quest for comeuppance through surrender to Jesus. Our brothers and sisters trapped in cycles of depravity are no longer crying out for help but are sold on postmodern cynicism and relativism for sale and freely offered through all media outlets. Where is Christ's free offer of salvation? It is under discarded hymn books, sitting beneath prosperity ministry videos, covered with voting guides and remains in dust-coated Bibles not yet out on DVD. The remainder of this book will explore this question by examining our present moral condition.

Chapter 2

NON-CLERICAL PROPHETS

Because your sins are so many and your hostility so great, the prophet is considered a fool, the inspired man a maniac.
–Hosea 9:7 b,c

We have grasped the mystery of the atom and rejected the Sermon on the Mount. –Omar Bradley

With the assurance that God's people know His will and opinions, Yahweh has routinely used prophets. Even though we are blessed to have His revelations and will contained in a handy book, God still dispatches truths to be revealed through men and women. It is especially ironic for the author raised within the dispensationalist tradition with its contortional attempts to render prophecy au courant; I found striking messages emanating from secular society which disdains even the notion of the prophecy (Nostradamus excluded). I was surprised to find "non-clerical prophets" messages aligning more with scripture and testifying against the condition of the nation more soundly than anything coming from the Christian prophetic conference and workshop cottage industry. Please read on.

Right Now, I look at it and I say, If I just draw a straight line from where we are now, one of three things has to happen. Either we have to have a major tax increase, taking back everything that happened under Bush and more, or we have to have drastic cuts in the core middle-class entitlement programs, basically. We have to have big cuts in Medicare and Social Security. If you ask me which one, the answer is God knows. But it's certainly going to be some kind of crash - Paul Krugman, Economist and New York Times Columnist[1]

The black religious experience defies monolithic interpretations. Black Americans can be found in all sorts of American religious organizations. Even though most blacks remain part of a Christian worshiping community, far more are seeking alternatives to the church. Islam is the fastest-growing religion in the United States, and its numbers are rapidly expanding among African Americans as well. With even Louis Farrakhan, leader of the Nation of Islam, increasingly leaning towards a more orthodox practice, Islam promises to hold a significant place in the black religious imagination. Hinduism and Buddhism also continue to make inroads into black communities in the twenty-first century, as globalization narrows the gap between

East and West. And as blacks seek to reclaim their African heritage, African-based religions like Candomble' and Santeria will still have a place on the black religious landscape. - Juan Williams, National Public Radio commentator[2]

Every group that wants to can anoint itself as God's chosen people. - Vernon Jarrett, retired columnist Chicago Tribune and Sun-Times[3]

The remarkable fact is that today so many Americans value marriage, get married and want their children to marry. Many often cohabit, but when a child arrives most get married. The ones who don't make their children suffer. But to many people the future means more cohabitation-more "relationships" -and fewer marriages. Their goal is Sweden, where marriage is slowly going out of style. -James Q. Wilson, political scientist at the University of Chicago[4]

It is now absolutely normal in many circles for young black men and women (and, for that matter, little black boys and girls) to refer to one another as niggaz and bitches and ho's. Doing well in school is frequently disdained a white thing. Doing time in prison is widely accepted as a black thing, and no cause for shame.

Few people are surprised to hear that a gathering at this party or that club degenerated into the kind of violence we used to associated with the O.K. Corral. Homicide, drugs and AIDS are carving the heart out of one generation after another, and suicide among blacks is on the rise.

My question is a simple one: When are we going to stop this? -Bob Herbert, New York Times Columnist[5]

Just because you beat a man doesn't mean you're going to change his mind! - Keisha Thomas, who shouted these words while protecting Klansmen from a violent assault by anti-Klan demonstrators[6]

In the past 10 years, we've seen the near total disintegration of black political and social leadership. That means the single largest influence on black America's self-image is popular culture, music, TV and films. - Aaron McGruder, political cartoonist[7]

They coddle them. They lie for them. They co-sign for them. Parents cover for their kids, even when their kids are dead wrong. And that's where the problems come in. They always say they want to give their kids more than they had. But sometimes more is not always better. Teachers quit because they can't teach these bad kids. Police officers can't patrol the streets anymore. We've dropped the ball. - Bernie Mac, comedian and actor on the state of African-American parenting [8]

We learned manners in home and in church. We stopped going to church and we stopped having homes, so we are no longer being civilized, no longer socialized - Eldridge Cleaver, radical and lifetime activist[9]

It no longer seems to me that we are preoccupied with education and intelligence. It's not cool, even sicker, we equate smart and intelligent with being white. Intelligence is white and uncool. Just because you're African-American don't mean anything you do is all right because you're African-American. - Spike Lee, film maker[10]

You know, I would really hate to be a young person right now. If we don't stem the tide now, the jobless percentage I'm talking about now will seem mild. And there is no serious planning going on for this. There will come a day when ignoring the poor is not an option. - William Julius Wilson, sociologist[11]

The black family has crumbled more in the last 30 years than it did in the entire 14 decades since slavery. - Julia Hare, sociologist[12]

Chapter 3

MORALITY BY NUMBERS

For the wages of sin is death. –Romans 7:23

Lest our feet stray from the places, our God, where we met Thee, Lest our heart drunk with the wine of the world, we forget Thee. –Black National Anthem, lines 28 & 29

It is standard operating procedure that whenever anyone outside the Black community lodges a charge or attempts to make a critique of any aspect of Black culture, unless it is praise they will be attacked if they are not Black. To illustrate this point consider David Change, a Taiwanese immigrant who after observing rap videos created *Ghettopoly*, a Monopoly spoof[1]. The object of the game, like Monopoly, is to dominate the board with crack houses as opposed to hotels and regular houses. Any game that celebrates immorality is deplorable to start, however Chang was attacked for perpetrating stereotypes and attempting to profit from them. Target identified, attacked and issue dodged as usual. SOP.

When other Blacks speak out about the ongoing troubles plaguing African-Americans and use statistics, they fall into one of two categories: popular conservatives pandering to White audiences (because the political affiliation causes most blacks to turn a deaf ear), and Black leadership calling for increased funding to solve the problem. And we cannot overlook pastoral use of statistics to make a point in a sermon. I shall do the same here with a variety of indicators. I challenge any reader to research each and verify the facts for themselves. It is important to re-emphasize that we are the second largest ethnic group in the population at 12.7%. Latinos are now the largest minority group at 13.4% of the U.S. population.[2]

Denominational statistics compiled by the New York Public Library indicate that 81% of African-Americans claim membership in Christian churches.[3]

According to *Target Market News*, Black buying power in 2002 was $631 billion dollars.[4] To put that figure into perspective consider the GDP of these African countries: Nigeria, Africa's fifth most populace nation $113.5 billion; South Africa $432 billion; and Egypt $268 billion. We spend more on consumer electronics ($3.2 billion) than Uganda's entire $3.1 billion dollar gross domestic product![5]

Census figures for the year 2000 show that slightly less than a quarter of Black Americans live in poverty. In 1960 the number was a staggering 55%.[6]

Fifty-six percent of abandoned babies were Blacks as opposed to 21% white and 14% Hispanic infants.[7]

About 53% of Black children are raised in single parent households with 48% living with their mother and a paltry 5% living with their father. Thirty-six percent of the children are raised in homes with a parent cohabiting with a non-parent. To put these numbers into perspective, 25% of Hispanic and 16% of White children live in single parent families.[8]

Black children make up 38% of those in foster care, followed by 37% White and 17% Hispanic. A staggering 45% of American children waiting to be adopted are Black. Of the children abused and neglected, 50% are White; 25% are Black, and 15% Hispanic.[9]

The median household incomes by race were: $55,521 Asian and Pacific Islanders; $45,856 Whites; $33,447 Hispanic; and $30,439 for Blacks.[10]

The Centers for Disease Control (CDC) reported that of those who died from AIDS, Blacks were 46%, Whites 34% and Hispanics

18%. Reports from the year 2000 indicate Blacks led the nation in HIV infection at 52%, followed by Whites 37%, and Hispanics at 8%.[11]

The CDC warned that the infection rate for the rest of the array of sexually transmitted diseases (STDs) was reaching an epidemic level. The gonorrhea rate for Blacks alone is beyond belief: 78% or 848.8 cases per 100,000 people. To put this into perspective, Native Americans have the second highest rate at 10%. The publication *Tracking the Hidden Epidemics 2000* stated that the STD rate for Blacks is thirty times that of Whites. "The disparity is due in part to the fact that African Americans are more likely to seek care in public facilities that report STDs more completely than private providers." Yet the report acknowledged that the reporting bias did not even begin to explain the dramatic difference. Sadly, Black Americans lead the nation in Herpes, HPV, Syphilis, Trichomoniasis, BV and Hepatitis B. [12]

In 1999, President Clinton ordered a study on the impact of expansion of casino gambling across the nation. The National Gambling Impact Study Commission found that "pathological problems, and at-risk gambling was proportionately higher among African Americans than other ethnic groups."[13]

The Office of Special Education OSEP, reports that "Black students with disabilities exceeded their representation among the resident population. The most striking disparities were in the mental retardation and development delay categories."[14]

Black youth accounted for 15% of the national juvenile population in 1996. Yet 40% were in residential placement due to serious offenses and another 43% were in custody in public facilities.[15]

The Federal Bureau of Prisons declared 40.4% of the inmates are black.[16]

Suicide among Black youth aged 10-19 increased 114% between 1980-1995. The Center of Disease Control hypothesized the increases were attributable to the breakdown of family as well as the growth of the Black middle class. In the case of the middle class youth, suicide represents an adoption of a mainstream coping mechanism.[17]

Out of the Black female population under 21, the U.S. Department of Health and Human Services estimated that 77.3% are overweight and or obese, and 60.7% of Black men.[18]

Research done by Yale University discovered Blacks tipped cab drivers the least and were most likely to stiff the driver. Blacks gave bigger tips to white drivers and were more likely to stiff Black cabbies. The report cited the findings as a possible reason why cabbies refuse to pick up Black passengers.[19]

Of the nearly 14 million arrests in the year 2000, 27.9% were Blacks. Blacks accounted for 48.7% of the murder arrests, 33.8% of the rape arrestss, 64% of the aggravated assault arrests and 53.2% of those detained for robbery. We also made up 30.3% of those arrested for crimes against children and family, 34.1% of the embezzlement arrests, and 34.1% of all arrests for fraud. I have included the Department of Justice Uniform Crime Reports Arrest data in the appendix for review.[20]

The Drug and Alcohol Services Information System issued the OASIS report in March 2003. The report is a compilation of statistics regarding those admitted to facilities for substance abuse treatment. Blacks comprised 30% of the adult admissions for marijuana compared to the 54% Whites who make up 70% of the population verses 12.7% Black.[21]

Blacks have the highest incident rate of lung cancer, largely attributable to smoking, and the highest mortality rate due to the cancer, surpassing all ethnic groups in the United States.[22]

It would be easy to dismiss this compilation of statistics as overly focused on collective depravity. Some would demand equal time to present the dignity embodied in Black America. For sure, as creatures crafted in God's image and honed by intense adversity, we are resilient, humorous, creative, intensely spiritual and so on. Our problem is that the spotlight has been resolutely focused on dignity ever increasingly in the past 40 years until the illusion of an absence of depravity has set in. Unfortunately, our distracted clergy have not kept up with the work of exposing the Black image to scriptures revealing the light.

Others may quickly offer these two explanations for the numbers. The first is the ongoing residual destabilizing effects of slavery. The second is ongoing efforts by racists operating clandestinely or openly in a series of conspiracies or historically learned behavior aimed at eliminating and exploiting Black people. These explanations are standard fare common to discussion among Black intelligencia or the patrons at the corner barbershop. Both explanations are problematic.

The residual racism/slavery effect does not account for the strength of the traditional Black family holding out from Emancipation to its societal peak in 1940s and kept pace with the White population through the 1960s. Scholars have attributed the post 1960's family destabilization to the welfare system, thereby implicating the Government even further as an enemy of the Black people. If we follow out that argument, we must remember Blacks were not forced to take welfare. Apparently, a collective greed infected us to overlook the fact that the welfare system required a father's abandonment in order to collect a state penance. The urge to sell out the family should have been widely resisted in that quarter as well as the collective exodus by upwardly mobile Blacks from class androgynous enclaves due to opportunities stemming from our newly won equality. The demise of the inner cities can be traced to the Black middle class' integration into mainstream class' exclusionary clustering model mirroring White America.

In both cases collective greed trumped common sense and historical precedent. Yes, we were impoverished but we survived together as families and as community. While I am not advocating desegregation and do believe that Black integration expanded the melting pot phenomena to all colored peoples rendering lopsided myth ecumenically viable, we cannot ignore the historical record.

Turning to the conspiratorial view in which Black America is continually under sustained attack by White America, be it cabal or collective; let us track that logic. As we know, the primary transmission means of HIV, the virus that causes AIDS, is unprotected sex and intravenous drug use. So despite an information avalanche and a conviction that AIDS is a genocidal plot, we find ourselves apparently incapable of modifying behavior to facilitate survival. Ironically, this is a validation of the racist tenet that Blacks are incapable of sexual restraint *not even to save our own lives.*

The San Jose Mercury News article *"Dark Alliances"* asserted that the CIA used funds generated from crack cocaine sales on American streets to facilitate support to anti-Marxist Contra rebels in Nicaragua.[23] Congress, in 1984, prohibited federal funding to the Contras. Gary Webb, the article's author, charged in addition to selling arms to Iran, that the drug sales were yet another avenue taken by the CIA to bankroll the Nicaraguan insurgency. The article set off a firestorm within the Black community with many, including Congresswoman Maxine Waters, declaring it the smoking gun.[24] Mainstream America, and especially those on the Right, dismissed the story and claim. Yet to dismiss this story outright is foolish as any historical survey of international intelligence services would reveal a full range of nefarious activities perpetrated against society's most vulnerable.

In Russia, the impetus for the Second Chechen War was fixed upon a terrorist attack on an apartment building housing poor Russian citizens. In recent years the bombing and the subsequent war against the Chechens has come under intense scrutiny by the Russian free press who began connecting the bombing to the KGB's reincarnation, the FSSB.[25] It must be noted that the Russian independent press has been subject to an ongoing intensive clampdown. Altruistically speaking, powerful men have always used the poor or minorities in plots for political gain, so to repudiate Gary Webb's "*Dark Alliances*" outright is historically short-sighted

Now what are we to think about "Freeway" Rick, the chief distributor of the CIA connected dope, and the armies of dealers, consumers, and assorted benefactors connected to the crack epidemic? Have Rick and the drug dealers been condemned as traitors, scoundrels, and collaborators in another genocidal design? No, conversely and perversely the drug culture has been heralded, mythologized, and trumpeted in artful venues. Rap music, movies, magazines, and even commercials have transformed a societal pariah into a cultural norm. Thugs as celebrity, lifestyle, and even romantic mates have been deemed acceptable and even desirable in publications such as *Ebony*.[26]

What does that say about a people? Jewish collaborators during the Holocaust were collectively despised and are repudiated today. French collaboration with Nazis is quietly ignored and unspoken out of a national sense of shame. Incredibly and unprecedently, we celebrate homegrown oppression and denounce outsourced injustice. Apparently, the White man is not the only one who speaks with forked tongue. This dualistic absurdity is not without precedent in America, for even today the rebellious tide that nearly sunk America is celebrated as upright heritage. Perhaps we should shelve out criticism of the Confederate banner as long as the flag of legitimacy is waved by us over Snoop Doggie Dog and Jay-Z's entertainment.

Which brings us back to the numbers; they exist as the documentation of immorality has gone mainstream within Black America. Instead of declaring a moral emergency, we declare conspiracy. Yet even in that declaration, the most unversed outside observer could not miss our co-conspiratorial actions. It is the nature of man to have his cake and eat it too. However, the biblical record is clear. Immorality leads to death, eternal separation from God, and everlasting punishment.

African-Americans may find the Apostle Paul's words insensitive, but even if he knew what political correctness was, he would still declare all humanity as slaves. Paul said as slaves we can live in only two conditions: slaves to sin resulting in death, or slaves to righteousness that leads to life. In our hard won natural freedom we have collectively chosen to be slaves: slaves to immorality. One bondage compounds another. Our slavery to materialism has demolished community and family. This collective thought process observed by two generations of youth has flowered faulty reasoning that legitimizes all methods (unethical or illegal) of accumulating wealth. The accepted practice of gaining wealth by other means had resulted in an expansion of criminal behavior and elevated incarceration rates. Our slavery to illegitimate sex has our minds gripped by pornographic themes in movies, print, language and our music. This sexual slavery has corrupted our bodies with AIDS and venereal disease and has the Black family hanging by threads on the verge of collapse.

Are we alone in this condition - no, but we lead the nation in a rush to bondage. Our politicians, athletes, businessmen, and entertainers trump announce our success to the world when below their feet our cities are in dust, both urban and suburban. I am unaware of an American equivalent to expressing intense mourning by wearing sackcloth and donning ashes. We are unfamiliar and averse to rending our clothes in like expression, but an honest contemplation of our moral condition would have us exploding in grievous cries for divine mercy. Repenting on our faces and knees is the only path to communal restoration.

Chapter 4

MEDIA AND CULTURAL PROPAGANDA

For the wisdom of this world is foolishness in God's sight. –I Corinthians 3:19

It's on the path you do not fear that the wild beast catches you. –African Proverb

The Twentieth Century's closing decades witnessed a new era of information synergism unlike anything the world has ever seen. This age of "media unlimited," as author Todd Gitlin termed it, is largely a commercial merge of television, print material, radio, and the internet mediums.[1] While politicians and others herald these days as plethora of empowerment for the individual, in reality the individual is nearly overwhelmed daily by an information tidal wave. This fourth estate largely serves corporate interest but it can be used to serve the state. Moreover, If Goebbels and the Nazi's could craft such an effective propaganda machine with newspapers, spectacles and movies, I shudder to consider the possibilities of our total information

49

age in diabolical hands. But what is propaganda really? Are we not exposed to it with every Jack-in-the-Box commercial, pop-up ad, junk e-mail, telephone call from MCI, and magazine ad?

Of our age Thomas de Zengotita writes, "Our minds are the product of total immersion in a daily experience saturated with fabrications to a degree unprecedented in human history. [2] He goes on to declare that never had people to cope with so much "stuff" and choices in kind and number.

Commenting from the Seventeenth Century Pascal thoughts were: It only needs one thing to go wrong to make us unhappy ... That is why men cannot be too much occupied and distracted, and that is why, when they have been given so many things to do, if they have some time off they are advised to spend it on diversion and sport, and always to keep themselves occupied.[3]

It is now the way of the world to partake heartily of the postmodern global marketplace by remaining constantly entertained and spending every dime available. Are we not subject to propaganda? For the Nazis Goebbels saw to it that every speech, presentation, appearance, film, article or story was crafted and calculated to manipulate the audience. He routinely created new words and mastered the sound byte, and with these tools the Nazis led their zealous population in a human rights' crime spree.[4] What does this have to do with Black America? Turn on a radio, watch a film preview, visit Blockbuster Video and you will see that Madison Avenue and Hollywood find Black Culture an effective tool to peddle wares and swell box office sales. Hollywood, the record industry and others have declared the Hip Hop/Hood culture to be the definitive and most profitable portrayal of Black life. While this is nothing new (read my paper in Appendix D), it is toxic propaganda foisted upon numb American minds. The choice of the Hip Hop/Hood image of Black life for worldwide distribution is part of the odious racial stereotyping lineage started centuries ago. The difference now is our people accept it, love the attention, and are committed to life imitating art.

Now we must discuss the use of the term Hip Hop/Hood culture, and to do so we must recall the 1970s blacksploitation films. After years of neglect Hollywood graciously decided to portray Black life on film, and unfortunately and deliberately (some argue), the subjects were pimps, prostitutes, drug pushers, and criminals. When a bonafide hero was allowed, he was not married and was usually the prototypical buck: an angry oversexed volatile Black man. These films were condemned and loved at the same time by the Black community. This archetype of film made a comeback as Hip Hop music was detoured to profitable depravity (gangster rap). Gangster rap was the aesthetic side of the drug culture's expansion during the crack cocaine era. Many street stars stepped out of the drug trade and into the world of art, their authenticity appreciated and venerated even today.

Liberal championship of relativism and conservative deliberate indifference and disdain of the Black poor created the conditions by which the Black underclass (post civil rights generation) embraced the new found attention generated by gangster rap. Living in the ghetto was now venerated as keeping it real. Ignorance and resistance to cultural evolution was (and is) resisted as new pride and interest (albeit long distance) was found in ghetto life. The new ghetto/hood lifestyle spread through the Black middle class youth, to Whites and across the globe. The link being the music—Hip Hop music.

Now let us look at some of the characteristics of the Hip Hop/Hood culture. We must recognize that this subculture arose out of anger and rebellion. The anger fostered in being left behind as Blacks integrated into mainstream societal acceptance and no longer being a fellow traveler on the road of American disdain. As the American economy shed manufacturing jobs since the 70s, inner cities and especially Black communities were stripped of employment opportunities and a tax base. Interestingly enough, the Whites were not the only ones fleeing to the suburbs. Those left behind did not feel or see that they had overcome. The camaraderie and brotherhood of segregation days disappeared as the upwardly mobile blacks were now able to earn the American dream. Scores lived on in a third world nightmare. The anger and frustration felt by the underclass continues to be transferred to violence, substance abuse and finally, a rejection of civilized living. Many may wince at the use of the term, "civilized living," but it is wholly appropriate. The values of the Hip Hop/Hood culture are anti-family, hedonistic, anti-intellectual, anti-authoritarian, and most definitely anti-religious. As a thirty-six year old I remember when rap music first came on the scene. As the genre blossomed there existed a vast variety of voices in the art. By the early 90s the major labels hedged their bets on gangster rap being the chief money-maker and it did as White youth sought to express their rebellion of being reared in divorce's wake.

We must be clear about the nature of gangster rap music. Simply put, gangster rap music is the glorification of the wholly evil and destructive drug culture. Yet, the Hood collectively claimed ownership because of societal disenfranchisement. The thug and thug life now celebrated represented an opportunity to sully the suit of Black respectability proudly heralded with each new public and private sector appointment. So as the new tale of Black life flowered in music, so did it in Hollywood with its genre of Hood movies. In art and in life, middle class Blacks would have to prove they were down and that they could keep it real. Even the author was not immune from signing on to this self-destructive foolishness. This quest for authenticity has us authentically mired in a cultural quagmire, all while we are losing moral ground gained from years of struggle.

Consider this: If a ten-year old starting around 1994 listened to Biggie Small, Tupac, Tha Dogg Pound and others day in and day out on a walkman while traveling; watched the videos on BET and MTV; and heard repeated recitation of sociological reasons and statistics declaring his future failure, why would he try? Has he not been made accustomed to Black on Black violence whether he lives in a suburb or in the ghetto? This young man, now twenty, has seen thousands of commercials whose impact has created the need for constant sensory consumption. Simultaneously, his ears have been saturated with messages of drug use, violence, misogyny, rebellion, excess materialism leadership, and general antisocial behavior interspersed amid ruthless catchy and infectious beats. Where in the realm of common sense would anyone expect upright, wise, and ethical decisions to be made by this person? We have long heard "you are what you eat" - and you are also what you think. Imagine the thoughts of this young man or young woman as we consider their role models and the amount of real time spent harvesting their warped ideologies.

Industry thoroughbreds such as Jay-Z, Ludacris, Lil' Kim, Missy Elliot and DMX are unwavering in their commitment to material excess; undeterred by any calls to examine the social impact of their lyrics and hold to the myth that only mature audiences are familiar with their material. Lil'Kim is hailed as a rap diva for aggressively marketing her sexuality (how original) and introducing the idea that there is no shame in getting paid for sex. Her siren calls to young women to shipwreck their lives on the sea of sexual immorality does not earn community ire. No, she is deemed legitimate talent worthy of a VH-1 *Behind the music* biographical documentary and Old Navy clothing commercials. Sociologists have started to weigh in rap music's effect on the young and still the clergy community stands quiet as Lil' Kim and Missy Eliot implore Black women[5] already being consumed by the STD arsenal to get their freak on, collect remuneration, and embrace the fiction that such action bears no relation to harlotry. Whereas the Nazi propaganda machine co-opted a society to engage in unparalleled serial murder, gangster rap and R&B musicians champion suicidal philosophies and behaviors while earning communal kudos for their talent. How many minds have been lost as these glorifications of sin remain unchallenged by the faith community? Why hasn't the firewall of the Gospel been declared as the only effective anecdote to this monstrous virus infecting the minds of our people?

Music artists' active and passive compliance with regimes bent on world market or cultural domination can lead to disastrous consequences. Just a decade ago, Hutu rebels with unsophisticated methods utilized radio to incite and direct a colossal genocidal massacre of the ethnic Tutsi population. Now, one must wonder, if a youth born in 1985 would spend his cumulative years drinking in rap music's dark self-hatred, egotistical, anti-social propaganda through his ears for a decade, what value system will stick into his mind? His mind is drenched in an overemphasis on negative influences in society, police brutality, a race-centered worldview, unbridled anger, the legitimization of criminal activity, incarceration presented as routine, reckless cavalier attitudes on sexuality, general hedonism, and a fervent disdain for any knowledge other than that pertaining to the street. This popular music is no longer attacked, but lionized as our creation. Our publications uncritically present gangster rap superstars as legitimate celebrities sharing the pages with Oprah, Bill Cosby, Denzel Washington and similar figures. *Jet* and *Ebony* are co-conspirators in their sending of mixed messages. Apart from Reverend Calvin Butts, the silence from the pulpits has been deafening. In the meantime, the streets flow with our blood during this internecine orgy of violence with a soundtrack and ideology provided by the record industry.

The second form of popular music, Rhythm and Blues or R&B, is as pitiful in its lyrical baseness. A quick survey of the top R&B hits at any given time reveals ballads celebrating sex, marriageless love, the glorification of unfaithfulness (creeping on the down-low), and more he said/she said relational disputes ad nauseam. Graphic language punctuates most lyrics and the Black church's collective response to popular music has been to mimic it, in and out of the church house. Would the masses that have given their lives to Christ because of Kirk Franklin driving a Hummer on stage of the Stellar Awards, please stand up? I will not denigrate nor limit the means by which God draws those to accept His Son, but we must honestly ask, is impersonating secular art really winning new converts to Christ? This discussion is thundering across the church world, and others such as Daniel Frankforter and John Frame have authored targeted works on the topic, so I will not belabor it any further.[6] We cannot forget that the Apostle Paul vigorously addressed the cultural encroachments within the Corinthian church. That phenomenon which occurred back then has not abated, it has increased.

Consider the dilemma, modern psychiatry has diminished shame and guilt. In addition to those voices, Missy Elliot and Little Kim tell the ladies to have no shame as they barter sex for resources. The call to be unashamed, if not proud, to sin occurs as a repeated theme in rap, on television, and in the actions of most movie characters. Conversely, the message from the pulpits has been tempered not to challenge or remind the masses we should be ashamed for our lawless rebellion and debasement of sin. The church's message must resonate with clarity. One should be guilty and ashamed of sin and wickedness. The church must also challenge the logic of street knowledge. Just what is this venerated street knowledge? The strong survive. It's dog eat dog out there. Trust no one. Cash is king. The Hood life is authentic living. The gangster lifestyle is now a legitimate career choice. R&B artists have cosigned on this absurdity by hailing gangster love as desirable.

Latina pop-superstar, Jennifer Lopez, was interviewed back when she dated Sean "Puff Daddy" Combs (now P-Diddy) and stated she loved dating bad boys because they make you feel safe.[7] Apparently she did not buy into her own rhetoric because she dumped Puff Daddy after a shooting occurred at a nightclub where they were hanging out. Even *Ebony* printed an article coaching women on how to date a badboy.[8] In the absence of common sense, how can a girl want a gangster love, and not expect to share a gangster's end? This is an example of the faulty thinking, foolish advice and unbelievable absurdity that is passed on through the popular media. How long will the church stand idly by and let postmodern Americans believe the only sages around are Judge Judy, Oprah, Dr. Phil and the daytime talk television crowd? We sit atop an inexhaustible supply of true wisdom that can be backed up with the supernatural power of the Holy Spirit for those who would believe and we say nothing. We must remember the Media has told kids that Biggie Small, Aliyah, Tupac and Left Eye were giants and artistic heroes. In reality they were no more than talented propagandists glorifying a legacy of shame, murder, and loveless sex; the legitimization of out-of-wedlock childbearing; and general rebellion against corporate morality. Their heroism lies in their success as capitalists and in their mantle of celebrity. They are hailed as champions of an industry which exploits most capably, and covertly serve the devil through seductive packaging of anti-Christian messages. No one tells today's starry-eyed youth odds of breaching the stratosphere of such fame are about the same as winning the Powerball jackpot. Many others are equally or more talented. They are just not picked.

As if the rain of antisocial influence is not enough flowing from music, we cannot forget television never faltering monsoon season. Recently, St. Louis celebrated the premier of channel UPN 46, hailed with pride as Black owned and operated.[9] Big names such as Mo'nique, Jerry Springer, coterie of local celebrities and the mayor attended the affair. A review of the UPN programming for the following week should have drawn a protest. UPN, while abundant with Black faces, is one of the most prolific networks for casual sex or sexual references and foul language outpacing even the notorious FOX network.

The Parents Television Council, a media watchdog group reported that UPN programming had an 188% increase in on-air foul language between 1998 and 2002.[10] *Girlfriends*, one of UPN's flagship programs, is a prime example of the postmodernist indoctrinizations that Americans are exposed to, and especially African-Americans since we watch more television than all other groups in America.[11]

Girlfriends is a Black cast version of HBO's cable hit *Sex in the City*. *Sex in the City* is nothing more than a soft-porn soap opera with major stars. The program's main characters are four upwardly mobile women who swashbuckle their way through men in search of good sex and maybe a relationship. *Sex in the City's* heroines are never perceived as sluts, prostitutes or loose women, instead they and the show are applauded for the portrayal of fashionable empowered women who are in control. *Girlfriends* is a clone of the show outfitted in black faces. Television restrains the graphic depictions of sex, but *Girlfriends* manages to capture the spirit and tenor of the original. The sinful lives played out in both shows are portrayed as glamorous and without consequence. This is the essence of the Devil's ideological psychological warfare campaign crystallized in postmodern culture. Man has been sold that the previous collectively condemned behaviors are now normal and without existential consequence. Satan has succeeded in repackaging the Garden of Eden message and selling it wholesale. Man is free to do as he wishes; ethics and law need only to be defined by man. Violators of the rule of law are deemed only as victims of faulty thinking, never immoral. Even the word immoral has been extracted from the public lexicon by the popular media and replaced by the milder variations of the term ethics. The root word "moral" of immorality begs to question whose morals, and asserts that there may exist a true set of morals which stands in stark opposition to the relativistic world view. Most of UPN's programming not only tows the larger cultural line, it stretches it out further.

UPN also airs the notorious *Jerry Springer, the Ellen Degeneres Show, Married with Children* reruns, *Angel* (a *Buffy the Vampire Slayer* spin-off) and *Cheaters*. *Cheaters* stands apart from the rest of UPN's fare for two reasons. First, *Cheaters* is UPN's only reality show and it is probably the only true reality show out of the whole genre. Secondly, *Cheaters* is one of the few shows on television in which viewers can see the pain inflicted by the offenders' depravity. *Cheaters* works like this: If a person is in a relationship in which they suspect infidelity, the show will put a team of private investigators on the case to verify the suspicions. The show builds suspense by showing the actions of the offender caught on video before they reveal it to the victim. Each segment builds to a confrontation, and in these clashes the true emotions are revealed that are absent from the whole of "reality TV." *Cheaters* allows the viewer to witness the rawness of mankind's depravity and see the shallow poverty of what passes today as modern love. *Cheaters*, UPN's only redeeming quality, illustrates the bankruptcy and failure of non-marital and premarital sexual norms ushered in by the Sexual Revolution. Despite this reality gem, the bulk of UPN's programming is pointless entertainment offering repetitive blueprints to civility's erosion through the use of base and vulgar subject matter. UPN has targeted Blacks as an audience and the preachers should be the first to let our community know that we are being harmed and not honored by their favor.

The Nielsen rating company has consistently reported that Blacks watch more television than all other ethnic groups in the United States. [12] This is obvious as one views an afternoon of BET and then takes a stroll through our neighborhoods. Television and movie's plot lines can be overheard playing out in the clubs and in the congregations. Our lives are imitating art in dress, action and value formation. This media propaganda has registered with great effect on the African-American mind. We have been re-enslaved for yet again commercial exploitation. Where are our prophets? Most are worried about their own profits. The freedom available to Black Americans to reject the images and live above the commercial mainstream legitimization of a stereotype should be shouted from the steeple tops. Until our prophets and preachers drop their search for fifteen minutes of fame, the media will continue to chart our destruction and document it on the nightly news.

Chapter 5

THE STATE OF THE INDIVIDUAL

When he saw the crowds, he had compassion on them, because they were harassed and helpless, like sheep without a shepherd.
–Matthew 9:36

The pace of life right now has been accelerated past our ability to live it. –Bruce Bendinger

Matthew 9:36 reports Jesus describing the crowds who gathered around him as harassed and helpless. Jesus' compassion grew as he gazed upon the shepardless sheep. The people of that age were living within a world less simple than we admit. It is difficult for contemporary man to consider the people of the New Testament era as living with layered societal complexity. Yet, they did under the oppression of extra-Levitical religious construct, beneath the rule of Roman colonists, and in the ongoing legacy of humanity's fall. Back then and as now, the individual suffers under a perpetual siege.

We live in the age of the global free market and that cult stands victorious over monarchism, feudalism, fascism, and communism. It has managed this feat with or without racism, sexism and religious approval. The cult of the free market has managed to draft psychiatry, sociology, and all manners of technology into its service. It is the individual who remains the last holdout. The free-will of man has yet to be conquered. Yet, still the onslaught grows daily. Out culture has transformed itself in submission to the cult. Few are able to grasp what has happened. Even fewer have the time.

Once the producers of goods realized that workers were needed more as consumers, the ad-men set about dismantling the image of the self-sufficient American. At the same time, the authority of parents was wrested away and crowned upon the experts. Insecurity was transfused into all aspects of life: family, dating, marriage, health and sport. An illusionary satisfaction is only permitted through conspicuous consumption. Christopher Lasch wrote in *The Culture of Narcissism* that posterity and the future are deliberately neglected to nurse individuals to an unceasingly affixiation on the here and now.[1] Within that context, momentary satisfaction reigns supreme.

While Lasch has described the American individual as a defined narcissistic archetype, Dick Keyes argues for two kinds of central figures of individuality: The New Victorian and the New

Romantic.[2] The New Victorian implements willpower and control in all aspects of life, and the Romantic plays the perpetual rebel supposedly living out true authenticity. Both are self-centered idolaters or narcissists as Lasch would argue. Keyes' New Victorian and New Romantic are readily identified in our culture. This odd couple is a pop culture staple appearing in every buddy cop movie, in the "fish out of water" films, in Congress, and starting for the Lakers. At the heart of these individuals and others like them is a grand charade, played with the sole purpose of convincing the world they are in control. Many other individuals unsure of their identities admire the New Victorian and New Romantic and spend lives mimicking and beating paths to these archetypes even through gender reorientation.

The foundation of our identity lies in our relationship with the creator. The severed path to our maker was restored by Christ heroic sacrifice. Even the most valorous actions by men to save fellow human beings do not translate into the saving of the soul. Yet, it is the folly of man to frame heroism primarily in fleshly terms. The truly honest reject the popular cultural grasp on denial, the denial of the need for salvation. The psychiatric community considers themselves generous by acknowledging religious belief as good for mental health. At the same time, their colleagues in the labs routinely publicize new evidence of our insignificance and dare to tread in areas exclusively the Creator's.

As technology has charged forward in areas such as genetic cloning, the religious community has failed to keep apace. The individual is buffeted in the breach armed with only sound bytes of explanations. He is declared significant and free but cannot ignore the feeling of insignificance in bondage to a nihilistic worldview. One routinely hears men or women declare themselves as being "basically good." This construct must be maintained to stave off vestiges of guilt as they wrestle through lives lived as offender and offended. Other devices are pursued robustly to drown out any pain and distract oneself from the fact they have no idea who stares back at them in the mirror. Humanity's ancient enemy makes full use of our culture to distract or eliminate the individual before they are in a position to surrender to God.

Our Savior waits patiently to restore the individual, give them purpose and identity. As so many are seduced into a life valuing style over substance, living and dying indifferent to the resolute purposefulness in each individual's creation, how can we believers be comfortable with this arrangement? As Dietrich Bonhoeffer asked, "Are we of any use?" [3] Do we not groan with Christ and feel his longing to spread the news of the Father's mercy? If we don't feel that, our union with Christ may be a mirage. If we are in union with Him then we would not tarry in our service to the Lord of the Harvest.

God created the individual for his own glory by investing of Himself. He remains the true soulmate of man. Unbelievably, popular culture markets the idea that such a union is possible with another human being. Many are sold on the idea they can find a localized god in flesh that will lead to lifelong contentment. This belief will lead to the diametric polar opposite: guaranteed future discontentment and interpersonal dissatisfaction. Never mind that its good for business-the romance business. No amount of money can buy the love waiting for the heartbroken individual. It is the preacher's job to let the people know that its real and free. Cost of subscription to online matchmaking service: fifty dollars a month. Cost of providing His son as an eternal soulmate to an individual: priceless. Like the Visa card motto, we must do likewise and take freedom to the individual everywhere He wants us to be.

Rodrick Burton

Chapter 6

EDUCATION

Fear of the Lord is the beginning of knowledge. –Proverbs 1:7a

Stupidity is a more dangerous enemy of the good than evil   .
–Dietrich Bonhoeffer

In 1997 in the Cleveland suburb of Shaker Heights, affluent Black parents demanded to know why their children were averaging a 1.9% GPA as opposed to the 3.45% GPA for their fellow White students. By all accounts, the Shaker Heights School District was using every method available to close the test score and grade gap. When the efforts appeared to fail, the parents and the school invited in an expert to study their dilemma.

The distinguished scholar, John Ogbu, was brought in from the University of California at Berkeley. As an anthropologist he studied how ethnic minorities coped academically in the United States and around the world. He and a team of researchers studied Shaker

69

Heights' schools, staff, students, and their parents for nine months. Then in a public forum he presented his findings. Promptly, he was attacked. He was called an Uncle Tom and derided as being culturally insensitive to Black Americans because of his African heritage. Black and White liberal scholars previously respectful of his work, levied charges of elitism, incompetence, conservatism, and even racism. Ogbu was deeply hurt and remains shaken by the whole affair until this day.[1]

What was it about Professor Ogbu's conclusions that made him a persona non grata to the Shaker Heights' Blacks? He contended that the Black student's failures were due to attitudes and subculture values that equate academic achievement as being synonymous with acting White. He discovered that most Black students valued leisure activities over success in school. Black students admitted and acknowledged they needed to make a modest effort with schoolwork but choose not to do so. When Ogbu inquired about their futures, many responded with certainty that they would lead successful careers as athletes and entertainers. It was clear to Professor Ogbu that the Black students were infected with an anti-intellectual worldview. Instead of accepting the findings and using it as an impetus for collective change, the parents vilified the messenger.

How can the parents who witness (and assist) their children's immersion in a popular culture which only applauds the entertaining and athletic Blacks actually be shocked that their youth do not value education? These same youth have constructed a hostile and exclusionary environment for children who attempt to academically achieve. The whole idea seems to be the epitome of a Klan inspired plot to destroy Black Americans, but it is not. This cancerous mentality that leads scores of Black youth down the path to poverty and jail sprung out of the Black Power Movement.

Proponents of the Black Power Movement rejected the whole of White culture for reasons that White academia ignored and sustained the ideological support of racial supremacy, so why would Blacks model the mainstream culture? This mantra was reintroduced during rap music's expansion in the early 1990s. Apparently to reject academic achievement is to don authentic Blackness and is an exhibition of Afrocentrism. The rappers and proponents of Afrocentrism would be hard pressed to find African or Caribbean natives opposed to academic study and achievement. Furthermore, the saddest aspect of this notion is it stands diametrically opposite the historical values that have brought Black Americans this far. Slaves learned to read in secret at great risk as well as the Whites who risked life and limb to teach them. Our faith and educational gains had been advocated universally throughout the Black community until our inclusion in the welfare state. Now our youth (not all) view school chiefly for its social aspect: a place to get dates, fashion new looks, develop gossiping skills, and prove their manhood through pointless conflicts. The new view finds school is a place for everything but education.

The media propaganda (discussed in Chapter 4) transmits an inexhaustive stream of messages aimed at youth to verify the anti-intellectual mindset. Since few schools teach critical thinking (colleges included), students are ill equipped to deconstruct the messages or resist them. Markets dictate the youthful cliché' to question authority - which is done with vehemence - but never to question their motives and methodology. A good case is that of Abercrombie & Fitch. Their clothes are the uniform of the 16-25 set. Abercrombie & Fitch had been rightfully criticized by a Christian activist for the sexual content found in their catalogues, but more recently they have come under fire for racist employment practices in keeping with their all- (insert White) American look.[2] Many youth are aware of the sexual controversy and purchase their clothes as an act of parental rebellion. These youth are unaware that Abercrombie & Fitch has no compunctions in exposing them to imagery depicting risky behaviors (group sex, bisexuality) and the promotion of a narrow definition of beauty found only in Whites. Abercrombie & Fitch are insulting and exploiting their customers, but unaware the kids buy it like hotcakes.

Public education is not what it used to be and never was what it should have been. In any case our public education system is the primary means of empowerment for the masses. African-Americans have developed an avowed distrust of the public educational system. It was in light of that pronounced reality, Professor Ogbu observed a cognitive disconnect among the Black parents in Shaker Heights,. On the one hand they expressed distrust of the school system and yet on the other they expected the system to do the total job of educating their children while they solely focused on building wealth.[3]

In the years prior to the Civil Rights Act of 1964, parents were assisted in child-rearing by the extended family, the neighborhood, and the church. Pastors, deacons, church mothers, elders and ushers taught, modeled, and expected civilized behavior. The Church's authority has been challenged and eroded by the popular culture. This wayward retreat is especially lamentable considering our peoples' long historical relationship within the church. The Civil Rights victory has turned out to be a key victory for the Devil as the Black masses replaced faith in God for faith in dollars. The new found faith has reaped monetary and social gain, but has bequeathed a legacy of rebellion and confusion manifested in the self-destructive ideologies of the youth.

As many of our children attend school with the intent of being stumbling blocks, can we be shocked or offended when Asians,

Hispanics, and Whites distance themselves from us? Is this racism? Prejudice? No, it is pragmatism. Public education has been watered down with the intention that no one will be offended by any textbook or lesson plan. The excessive striving for political correctness has ultimately offended students with their blandness.[4] Adding insult to injury, school districts are forced to squander funds on a standardized test orgy; made to do more with less as selfish empty-nest baby-boomers demand lower local taxes; and must battle the drive of religious interests to redirect public funds to parochial coffers. Is it a wonder students receive any education at all? Yet within this context we would allow our children to be agent provocateurs and inhibitors to that already burdened process. The Bible provides an answer to the question as to why our children nationally test lower: Fear of the Lord is the beginning of knowledge, but fools despise wisdom and discipline (Proverbs 1:7). In order to escape fool's valley we must return to the grass roots of knowledge.

Chapter 7

LAW AND ORDER

Everyone must submit himself to the governing authorities, for there is no authority except that which God has established. –Romans 13:1

Whether the knife falls on the melon, or the melon on the knife, the melon suffers. –African Proverb

Every so often the collective Black leadership issues a warning about incarceration rates as evidence of racism. The Black clergy sound off in unison and support. The rates are declared evidence of the racist court system when ironically the clergy should be pointing to the high numbers as evidence of a moral epidemic. Such an admission however would mean bearing responsibility. Has anyone ever analyzed the absurdity of this proclamation? Is a federal judge about to sentence a mid-level drug dealer supposed to free him or be more lenient because of the imprisoned Black multitude? Of course not. The same Black leaders deriding the state for locking up so many brothers begged the government for help during the crack epidemic. To attack

75

the state for locking up offenders while mutually demanding justice and safety in the community from a government derided as morally bankrupt is an exercise in illogical dualism. Simply put, this is pure nonsense. This line of reasoning is the most problematic when proclaimed by Black ministers.

Paul is clear in Romans 13, when he commands believers and nonbelievers to be submissive to civil authorities instituted by God to govern, administer his justice by proxy, and restrain anarchy. Do the U.S. civil authorities have a distressing history of prejudice dealing with Black America? Yes. Does that give us a free pass to disobey the law? Never! Our prolongation of the eternal victim status comes at the expense of our own safety and civilization. The statistics bear out we are our own worst enemies. An article in *Soldier of Fortune* magazine related the fact that White cops working in Black communities are laying back on their jobs in the face of routine communal charges of brutality. [1] Of course police brutality is criminal and must be clamped down upon, but do we expect hardened street hustlers who have no regard for the community who cries out on their behalf to be deterred with coddling? Romans 13:2 regards these individuals as rebels who have brought man's judgment upon themselves. There is an incredible disproportion of Blacks arrested, convicted and incarcerated as I have noted in chapter three. This is due to the criminal action of free will. Does racism's residue mean some Blacks are receiving comparatively longer sentences? Undoubtedly yes. Are some innocent? Yes, as are some Whites, Latinos, and Native Americans. It is the retention of the "we-do-no-wrong" fiction that has ill served the community by challenging the assumption that law and order are negotiable in civilized society. Ages before the sociologist, God recognized that circumstance and desperation drives some to criminal behavior (Numbers 35:11, Joshua 20:2, Proverbs 6:30-31), but the situation does not pardon the sin. Our clergy should trumpet that fact loudly. Who has not heard that "two wrongs don't make a right?"

Instead of being repudiated, the players and hustlers have earned hero and role model status. The pimp and his junior league companion, the player, are no more than narcissistic parasites and exploiters of women. How dare we deem their behavior tolerable by mimicking their vernacular? The pimp and player are the prototypical stereotype of oversexed criminality that was ascribed to all Black men by racist doctrines for hundreds of years. Now in movies, music videos, magazines (including *Ebony*), and other music venues, this behavior is seen as common to the Black cultural experience. And as Eric Strosser pointed out in *Reefer Madness*, when immoral or taboo behavior becomes mainstream the waves reverberate throughout society eroding other pillars of civility.[2]

When Black leaders attempt to win points among the constituency by proclaiming incarceration rates as evidence of racist America, it does nothing for those imprisoned or their families. Ex-convicts have always faced challenges in finding employment. The litigation-excessive character of our society has made this especially arduous. Employers are fearful of being sued by negligent hiring practices if any negative incident occurs surrounding the ex-convict or parolee. This problem is easily addressed by introducing legislation holding employers harmless in such cases. This legislation is not a priority since congressmen or senators would not dare risk doing anything that could be construed as being soft on crime. Instead of waving incarceration rates on a flagpole, Black political leaders should be removing ex-offenders' barriers to work and Black preachers should be laying some scriptural barriers down to deter the offending behavior.

The fallout from September 11 caused yet another crisis for ex-offenders seeking to reintegrate society through gainful employment. Employers in a patriotic zeal sought to improve security and denying terrorist employment by intense criminal background checks on current and potential new hires. Employers have deterred scores of ex-convicts from gaining employment with these measures. Operationally, most terrorists use cover identities free of arrest records in order to carry out their missions without drawing attention. No one is interested in addressing the unintended consequence of the elevated security measures which ironically leads to more garden variety street terrorism perpetrated by ex-convicts turned recidivist due to no employment opportunities. The Black community with its multitudes locked away, one day to be released, is silent on this issue. Christ declared those who aid the prisoner are serving His interest. The Black ministers should have two roles to play in addressing law and order in the community.

They must demand an uncompromised morality for all and submission to civil authority. Civil Rights era civil disobedience should be put in its proper historical context. Law breaking rooted in immorality will not be tolerated. Only if you get arrested for preaching the gospel will we bail you out. The church should campaign tirelessly to evangelize, train, mentor, and get ex-offenders work.

The pastors should be leading the faith community and others in challenging criminal encroachment in our communities. We are to hate what God hates—evil! Collectively, we confronted a massive culturally integrated state-sanctioned apartheid. With prayers, songs, and collective unity, onslaughts of armed troopers, vigilantes, Klansmen and throngs of hostile citizens were defeated by the power of God's love for justice. Yet, now we have surrendered whole communities to criminal elements who revel in their rebellion and have been glamorized by popular culture.

The Bible in both testaments heralds the actions of the good and calls to those who would serve God and Christ to emulate their divine goodness. Conversely, the marketers have deemed that bad is good. The bad boy image gets the lion's share of attention now. White yuppies are in the midst of a trend to model themselves after Hell's Angels bikers. Leather and Harley Davidson motorcycles are all the rage. Soft-as-cotton Baby-Boomers are getting their kicks riding around appearing dangerous. With African-American generations X and Y, the thug look and thug life are prominent popular trends. Their foolishness has led to society treating more Blacks as potential thugs. This is the dirty little secret and true reason for police profiling. The cops aren't offending us - we are offending ourselves as we retain and continue to promote this thug life foolishness.

Our folly serves the Devil's destructive purposes as each degree of separation, every league submerged in sin, handicaps the believer and convinces the unbeliever that a union with Christ is impossible. Thereby, the prison walls that surround Attica, Leavenworth, Angola, and Folsom prisons extend outward surrounding even the hearts of those who would never see the inside of such places. It is time to continue the Master's work of setting the captives free, and on the way we must also find ex-offenders gainful employment.

Rodrick Burton

Chapter 8

MARRIAGE AND SEX DEVALUED

Marriage should be honored by all, and the marriage bed kept pure,
for God will judge the adulterer and all the sexually immoral.
–Hebrews 13:4

Central to our discussion of the moral state of Black America is the core condition of the nuclear family. The authoritarian scientific sterile tone of the term "nuclear family" may seem dated, as it has fallen out of use while sin has forced Western societies to open up the term "family" to broad interpretations. Yet, when coined by the sociological community, chances are they had no intention of introducing a term that squarely aligned with God's view. When we hear the word nuclear, we think powerful as in nuclear bomb or elemental as in nucleus. Both are appropriately applied to what the family unit is. Family is the amalgam that holds and has held all functioning societies together. The union between man and woman,

83

marriage, is at the heart of the family, which is exactly the way God ordained it to be.

In Genesis 2:24, we witness the first ordination: The marriage of man to woman. The unity of one flesh, the sexual union,[1] has been sacredly reserved for the marital relationship without shame. It has been an indicative of the Western human experience that shame and guilt be assigned to the sexual union. Whereas the only shame or guilt surrounding sexual relationships should naturally occur if they take place outside of the marital context. Yet, that inversed history came crashing on its head through means of revolution - the Sexual Revolution. Science, historical gender oppression, and misinterpreted biblical religious sexual dispositions collided in the 1970s. As a generation rebelled against the collective lies and failures of a society called to explain its duplicity, it unwittingly offered further assistance to the serpent in his cosmic campaign against humanity, which as we know originated in the garden.

The Sexual Revolution vociferously declared sex good for the people. It was a natural human expression that, like our freedom, shouldn't be repressed or denied by any willing participants. Just like that, with the assistance of a young multi-tentacled media, sex was wrenched from its familial roots and declared public domain. Homosexual sex is declared natural as well as other deviant varieties such as sadomasochism, bondage, and bisexuality. Technological advances in contraceptives and legalized abortion presented new options during the revolution that previously were barriers. The popular culture exploded in an orgy of celebration for the wide distribution of a restricted fruit. The orgy continues today with more and more partners joining in. Despite recent attempts to refocus the sexual dialogue back to marriage, Pandora's Box is open. Round two has transpired between the serpent, man and woman. Postmodern men and women have devoured another fruit from the tree and have declared it theirs to grow, market, cook and eat. In this second ghastly round of arrogance, we have decided that sex not only belongs outside of God's mandate that it remain in the confines of the marital unit and be the proper method for family construction, but that family can exist and be created without marriage.

Quietly under the guise of assisting couples, fertility science and the free market have enabled anyone desiring children the means to do so. Invitro fertilization, surrogate mothering, sperm preservation/donation, and genetic cloning all serve as venues for further familial destabilization. Ironically, the scientific community has affirmed God's divine design, by asserting to the public that the best conditions for child rearing are within the dual sex, two-parent system.[2] Unfortunately, their declarations ring impotently in our narcissistic culture. The path to organic cultural restoration still exists and only exists through the submission to the divine will. God loves families. He made them! We must undermine the ongoing satanic plot that has the view of the world aligned with the debauched desires of the flesh to experience sex in a context of our choosing. To do this means getting back to basics and reinstituting marriage as the only accepted norm for sex and family. Now let us consider what Paul said in Ephesians 5:37:

"But among you there must not be even a hint of sexual immorality, or of any kind of impurity, or of greed because these are improper for God's holy people. Nor should there be obscenity, foolish talk or coarse joking, which are out of place, but rather thanksgiving. For of this you can be sure: *no immoral, impure or greedy person-such a man is an idolater - has any inheritance in the kingdom of Christ and of God.*" (NIV, italic emphasis mine.)"

Postmodern values have erected new asherah poles as tempting to modern Christians as the originals were to the Hebrews of ancient Israel.

The Hebrew was consistently seduced to participation in fertility rites practices within the idol worship in the region. The asherah poles God declared an abomination were a combination of totem poles and a campsite brothel. The onsite illicit acts of sex were fervently believed necessary to appease the Near-Eastern pantheon of

86

gods in order to insure crop growth. In those times societies were agrarian and worries about crop failure were similar to our concerns about economic stability. For the Hebrews to participate in such rites was an especial affront to Yahweh who revealed himself in truth and visible power on numerous occasions. God instituted true worship practices meant to be a model to the world through Israel. His law was known to all, yet still the temptation to commit collective sexual sin caused numerous Israelites to stray. God's righteous wrath followed prophetic warnings and calls to eliminate the asherah poles and the false worship associated with them.

Tragically, even under the New Covenant of grace, we find ourselves in a similar situation. Modern world sexual mores declare sex to be free for all, necessary for proper health maintenance, and to reject any religious voices calling for restraint by charging that such voices were responsible for its former constraints. All prohibitions must be discarded as individuals are afforded the right to express their sexuality to its fullness is as American as apple pie and voting. Though monogamy is paid lip service, great sex is expected to be part of every liaison, affair, period of dating, and relationship be it female-male, male-male or female-female.

This cult of sexuality saturates our lives as markets, Hollywood, musicians, comedians, and everyday people looking to make an honest or dishonest buck in America utilize sex blatantly or implicitly. On the new morality Eric Schlosser writes:

For almost two millennia pagan and Christian views of the body have remained in conflict, their rivalry expressed in various forms. But the old systems of moral authority have been replaced by a new one. The rules that govern sexual behavior are no longer determined by the pronouncements of stoic philosophers, high priest, martyrs, or saints. Democracy has increasingly granted freedom of choice in matters of sexuality, while the free market ministers to consumer taste.[3]

Schlosser goes on to chronicle pornography's transition from the underground economy throughout America's history to its mainstream debut as the major hotel chains now provide porn on demand in rooms across the nation. Mainstream media companies such as Echostar, DirectTV, AT&T Broadband and AOL Time Warner have muscled into the lucrative business of providing subscribers pay-per-view adult entertainment.[4] The new asherah poles are providing fertile fields of dollars for America's corporations.

We can see on newsstands, in movies, and on television how the sinful buds nourished during the Sexual Revolution have grown into robust vines that choke out the idea of monogamy and portray such a notion as an implausible relic of a bygone era. Popular mores expect boys not to even consider virginity and instruct girls to wait no longer than to the arrival of "the right time." Daytime Television's Soap Opera immorality is eclipsed by the talk shows aired at the same time. A child sick at home from school can hear a Ricki Lake guest defend infidelity on grounds that his partner/boyfriend/spouse was sexually ineffective. He can see Maury Povich surprise couples with paternity tests confirming or denying the human byproduct of illicit unions. The child can turn on BET and deduct what "Pimp Juice" is by the effect Nelly is having on the scantily clad vixens grinding suggestively in his music video.[5] Soap operas, in an effort to keep up, have taken plot lines over the top with marriage being synonymous with infidelity. The media's entertainment reporting assists the television and film industry, not by its useless box office sales recitations, but by extending plotlines from the screen into reality by broadcasting celebrity sex lives. One glance left or right in the grocery checkout line offers big, colorful attention grabbing reading enabling any adult or first-grader to keep up with which entertainer or actress is sleeping with whom or has been cheated on. Worse still, in 1998, the government released the Starr Report to the public.[6] The sexually explicit documentation was spread throughout every media outlet by a political party which claims ownership of family values and Judeo-Christian ethics.

It is from within this dome of omnipresent sexuality American Christianity has quietly surrendered to the new asherah poles with an apparent belief that grace is not sufficient and that Ephesians 5 can be ignored and cast into the trash can along with Christ's teachings on divorce. Church attending Christians promote and routinely send their offspring to secular colleges with the naïve belief they will resist the cult of collegiate debauchery with its standard issue of excessive chemical and sexual experimentation now instituted as the unrecognized portion of the curriculum. Some of these same Christians are amazed at reports about Canaanite parents sending daughters off to do their year's service at the base of the asherah pole. The belief that their god's demands for the girl's stint as religious prostitutes to ward famine off the land surpassed the Canaanite parent's personal anguish in contemplating the daughter's fate. Those ancient actions replay themselves every fall as Christian parents pack their children off to serve at new asherah poles so they can get a high paying job upon graduation, enabling the Believer to cast his boast about the success of their offspring at the office water cooler. And in keeping with postmodern culture, Christian parents are advising their sons and daughters to postpone marriage like everyone else—naively believing they will maintain virginity until marriage. The implicit message conveyed is that nothing, including morality, is to supercede the drive for material gain and the world's recognition. Sadly, the American

Christian's capacity to forget and ignore Christ's teachings equals the ancient Israelites and their tragic amnesiatic disobedience.

Black Americans have fought intensely throughout American History against the characterization that we are oversexed and subordinated to such a debauched nature. However, since 1964 the yoke of Christian values has been shelved and replaced with the postmodern sexual attitudes. The decision to trudge with the yoke is not enough; instead we must charge like a racehorse. The Black family jockeying along has been unsaddled, dragged behind through the dirt, and precariously hangs on with one foot in the saddle as the horse runs away from the finish line.

From our entertainers to our politicians and our preachers, we find postmodern sexual values modeled for all observing generations. This is especially troubling considering 81% of Blacks claim to be Christians. Our awareness of what is said to pollsters to make us collectively look good far outweighs our knowledge of scripture. Christ's truth and His messengers charged with sharing that truth waiver on commands to avoid sexual impurity and reserve sex for the marriage bed. We've bent on that truth leaving many to question the validity of the claim of biblical inerrancy as they see the clergy behave like everyone else. We are declaring the awesome power of the Holy Spirit to be insufficient to sanctify the individual. So many of us have failed to even resist the Devil's lascivious temptations in the resignation that "boys will be boys." This surrender to the new sexual mores bolsters the falsehood championed by the antichrist declaring the crucifixion and resurrection as impotent mythology. How dare we impugn the inestimable cost paid by our Savior? How dare we contradict his sacred words and disrespect his precious name declared exalted by God?

And yet we do, and we are suffering for it. God is merciful even in his correction. The numbers in chapter three could be far worse. We are also suffering as our prayers go unanswered, in the debasement and stagnation of the Black church. Despite the boast of our mouths, God has lifted our skirt and has exposed our nakedness to the nation. We are too busy bragging, demanding satisfaction for slavery, or begging to notice the laughter and scorn emanating even from those truly African. The failure by the church to stand firmly and resist the onslaught of new sexual values weakened its message. Even today, in light of their own record many pastors tread lightly or hesitate to call for sexual purity in the fear of offending congregations by appearing to be hypocrites. Hypocrisy is easily overcome by an open and honest admission and refraining from sinful behavior. The pastor who condemns his own depravity first carries the weight of integrity in his message.

As Black Americans, in light of our struggle to attain family (and even basic marital rights), the present state of the family should be cause for an intimate groaning. Marriage and family stability were denied during slavery. Emancipated slaves pursued marriage and family with a determination layered with aspirations of cultural reconstruction, collective healing, and the opportunity to follow biblical instruction regarding the family.[7] The quest to construct the Black family also arose as a protective measure. It is easily and persistently forgotten that the multiplicity in shades of skin tone visible among African-Americans is the forensic historical evidence of the sexual exploitation Blacks suffered at the hands of Whites during slavery up to the Civil Rights Era. Placing traditional cultural control on sex and family meant erecting a firewall against that bitter reality.

So we see historically that marriage and family are, or rather was of enormous importance to Black Americans. Under the direction of the Black preacher, Blacks were strongly exhorted to abstain from sexual sinning. Not only for the primary reasons, holiness and obedience, but as a matter of pride. Let me clarify this pride. This was not the self-righteous pride exhibited by religious people of any stripe, but a pride inspired by a need to repudiate the racist propaganda used to characterize Blacks as subhuman creatures devoid of intellect and restraint. The ongoing oppression continually demanded a justifying ideology to construct permissive conditions for that purpose. For that

93

reason African Americans were subject to dehumanization as long as mainstream America accepted the subhuman differentiation. Humans have always used this methodology to wage war, exploit, or subjugate targeted groups of people. Consequently, from early days the Black woman was described as sexually voracious—conveniently justifying any slave master's rapacious appetite or suppressing any guilt over forced breeding. Hence the birth of the infamous expression: "she wanted it." That was label number one. Label number two was ironically a necessary spoiler to prevent any such experimentation by White womanhood. The Black male was as equally voracious as the Black female, totally incapable of controlling his desires for sex (and preferably outside his race).

In the mid 1800s James Hammond was a South Carolina Congressman, Governor and slave owner. He was well known for his death penalty for abolitionist advocacy and was a champion of the infamous Patroller system essential to maintaining the police state security in the slave territories. Interestingly enough, Hammond, a professing Christian, vigorously advocated the suppression of Black Christianity, unless led by White ministers. He believed the carnal untamed sexual nature of Blacks alone justified the need for slavery. This position was espoused by a government official, landowner and pillar of society who, according to historian Martin Duberman, had sex with his nieces, daughters, his slaves and two men.[8] Slavery was a moral corrupter for all involved and the legacy for blaming the victim for it gained steam centuries ago and is continuing on unto this day.

I used the Hammond illustration to make the point about the insidious and monolific use of sexual stereotypes about Black Americans. This is why it is especially appalling that after centuries of efforts spent countering such depictions from pulpits and in practice to see the contemporary Black man and woman shamelessly embracing the stereotypes with enthusiasm. Postmodern sexual mores have been adopted, embraced, and advanced by Blacks to the extent that other groups are following our lead in wrecking the family unit. Now as sociologists, cultural critics, and historians trace the deconstruction of the family to Whites in the late 1950's, however today it is most apparent among African Americans.

Recently *U.S. News and World Reports* documented the sexual activity of preteens and early teenagers.[9] As alarming as that report was, it was not until media icon Oprah did a show and an article in her magazine that the issue gained national attention.[10] This shocking revelation produced a brief ripple effect in the form of other outlets doing a few similar stories, but as with many topics circulated by the media, it quickly fell off the national radar screen. Such an outcome is to be expected as postmodernism's relativism stymies the discussion of addressing actual root causes. To do so would tread into

95

the off limits waters of morals, which lie too close to the depths of religion. Such a swim is heartily rejected. In the articles the best parents could do was to get their sons and daughters to admit it was too soon as they offered advice to wait until the right person comes along. Even the suggestion to wait for marriage is relegated as too close to religion or hypocritical in light of the mother's sexual history. It seems ridiculous to think that parents would honestly believe children bombarded by sexual imagery on television, radio, in magazines, and in movies would not be seduced to find out what all the hoopla is about.

Marketers have long extrapolated sex as a sales tool, but today it is to the extent of iconic saturation. On November 19th, 2003, CBS aired Victoria's Secret Fashion Show for the second time.[11] The network had no qualms about presenting a sex-centered infomercial but squeamishly and cowardly pulled a biopic about Ronald Reagan for fear of offending conservative viewers.[12] Sadly, no second thought was given for overt sexual exploitation to merchandise racy skivvies on prime time but much more thought to maintaining mythological status for figures in American history.

Rutgers University is spearheading the National Marriage Project. It is a comprehensive study into the social indicators of marital health and well being over the past four decades. In their report, *Unions 2003*, they discussed the poverty of connectedness:

"The weakening of marriage has contributed to a new kind of poverty among the young. It is a poverty of connectedness. Four decades of persistently high levels of marital disruption and nonmarriage have taken a toll on children's primary sources of emotional nurturance and security. Parent-child, and especially father-child ties, have become more turbulent, insecure, and anxiety filled as a result."[13]

Christ defined this universal condition when in Matthew 9:36 he described the crowds as harassed and helpless. His words then defined this generation now. Battered and leaning like Pisa's famous tower, they await the crash as the marital foundations quietly slip away.

Where is marriage going? It is falling into the hands of those it does not belong and it is being taken to places it was never intended. Gays in search of the ultimate legitimacy have campaigned for legal and societal recognition of their abnormalcy since the pitched battles for gay rights in the 1970s. The ultimate legitimacy for their outlaw lifestyle would mean dollars. If America is going to view two individuals that nature affirms are not candidates for marriage to be eligible for benefits and tax breaks, then the two good buddies sharing a room together at state college should be eligible too. No one, straight or gay, is taking a common sense look at the legal Pandora's Box that gay marriage will open up.

Heterosexuals, following Hollywood's lead, view marriage as the domain for soulmating. The soulmate view detours marriage away from the path to raising and sustaining the family and boomerangs it back to the familiar narcissistic self. The belief in soulmates is not born out of an idea that God has the right spouse for the individual, but that there exists an individual is, as Depeche Mode sang it, a personal Jesus. The American narcissists wrapped up in a personal idolatry expect another finite human being to provide all their spiritual and sexual needs. Rutgers concludes that this selfish view of marriage, coupled with aggressive marketing by the bridal industry through movie and television plotlines featuring grand weddings, account for the modest recent spike in marriages.[14] Today the idea of a wedding is hot. Marriage as social responsibility is not.

For Black people, the topic of marriage holds monumental significance, as yet new poverty of connectedness sweeps a wider swath through our children. Statistics show that our women are the most likely never to be married and most likely to raise children in that context. If the Black popular subculture deems study and intellectualism as White characteristics, will marriage be next? How can we stem the tide washing away our social piers and leaving cumulating toxic garbage our beach of humanity? We must return to the Gospel introducing some and reacquainting others with our Savior. History can be reconciled with His story. From there we can begin to address this problem through service - service to Jesus Christ through the family. With eyes wide open to the light, then many will be ready to drink the scriptural and empirical data on marriage.

Once Black men understand the eternal relevance of today's action, they will turn their hearts to Christ mournfully repenting for the catastrophic neglect of family. Our preachers must broadcast the fearsome reality of 1Timothy 5:8 where believers who neglect their families are denounced as worse than unbelievers. This is not such a big deal if one subscribes to the popular heresy of universalism where everybody makes it to heaven someway, even Sadaam Hussein and Bin Laden. The Bible does not affirm any view of the sort. Churches must clarify and preach eternal destinies. Research done by the Barna Group finds popular secular beliefs on the afterlife have gained widespread acceptance among Christians.[15] How can we appreciate Christ if we don't know what He saved us from and what he promises us? Black men must be informed that indifference to family rate eternal judgment, and worse for those claiming to be Christ's own.

The problems that plague our community are complex and rooted in effects of a depraved history. God's solutions for man's problems are simple. They start with a simple surrender and absolute honestly in repentance. The solutions, His solutions, lie within an inquiry: An inquiry of the Lord. Then we must simply wait and listen. He answers, acts, or asks us to act. It is that simple. He is our simple salvation for the sweet by and by, but also the present.

As I conclude this chapter on sex and marriage, the Christian acceptance and practice of premarital sex, this assumption of normalcy holds many ministries in check from calling congregations to chastity and youth to virginity. The failure to do so is a failure to truthfully communicate the Gospel. Whomever we first sexually unite with is considered by God as our wife. Depending on whether we marry that person or continue to plot a sexual history determines if we are properly married or fornicators. And while society may advertise the need for sexual experience and encourage experimentation, we are condemned under divine law. God created the virginal affinity for the husband only, not the traveler on the sexual superhighway. Despite feminist and assorted postmodernist claims, sexual relations generate profound feelings. These cannot be ignored, and this was the greatest miscalculation of proponents of the Sexual Revolution. One biproduct of the revolution was the resulting war of the sexes. Protocol for the war of the sexes dictates each side uses sexuality for gain *without emotional attachment*. This is further evidence of man's ignorance in the face of divine design.

Even my grandmother marveled at the simplicity in God's call for monogamy. Now Grandma watches a fair amount of television like many seniors, especially talk shows. On most weekdays Maury, Montel, Ricki Lake or Jenny Jones will have guests bemoaning sexual betrayal or defending betraying behavior. Too often it is the betrayers' mental (and times active) catalog of sexual experiences that they say cause them to seek better sexual partners. Well, Grandma says it's like home-cooking. "If you only eat what's in the pot at home, it'll always be the best." As individuals move into relationships with Samsonite bags of sexual history, the best possible mate may be discarded due to historical comparison. God knows what is best. Preachers preach chastity. If you sinned, admit it and reclaim the moral high ground seized by the Savior. Compromise will not bring God's blessings. Due to the times the new asherah poles may be here to stay, but through Christ with the power of the Holy Spirit, we can topple the allegiance to the asherah poles starting with us and spreading throughout America.

Rodrick Burton

Chapter 9

THE STATE OF BLACK CLERGY

Those who guide this people mislead them, and those who are guided are led astray. –Isaiah 9:16

He that cannot obey, cannot command. –Ben Franklin

I have discussed our moral state in historical terms and with statistical evidence, but now we must discuss the issue of responsibility. The blame falls squarely at the feet of those who have been commissioned to shepherd the flock: the preachers. There is no need to deconstruct the historical record to explain why Black clergy hold a higher position of influence within the Black community. The reason is simple: since slavery they have been the only leaders we had. Obviously, as progress and Black influence was allowed to blossom, a variety of other leaders have appeared. We cannot forget that it was God's use of a Christian preacher, Martin Luther King, Jr., to usher in a new era and new found opportunity that benefited not only Blacks, but all Americans. With 81% of our population claiming Christianity through church membership, the Black preacher still carries tremendous influence. It has been the pastor who has defined acceptable behavior and has pushed, cajoled and exhorted our people to collectively overcome the ill will shown us. So what happened? This chapter will attempt to answer that question.

Criticism of the Black clergy is nothing new. Charles Hamilton, author of *The Black Preacher in America,* reported, "complaints have been divided into four categories-those who are materialistic, nonintellectual, authoritarian or politically non-involved.[1] Contemporary preachers have made gains (many superficial) concerning intellectualism. Political activism is hit or miss. Authoritarianism remains a problem and materialism has spread like cancer among the clergy. The newest and most pressing problem is the failure to preach the uncut gospel in addressing sinful practices gone mainstream.

Abortion is seen as an issue driven by the White Conservative/fundamentalist Christians. The historic circumstances originate during the fourth failure of American Christianity. After discrediting itself in the eyes of the young Baby-Boomers for resisting and denouncing the Civil Rights Movement, American Christianity needed a rallying issue to regroup the faithful. Feminist and Sexual Revolution proponents scored a victory for postmodern values when in 1973 the U.S. Supreme Court legalized abortion. American Christianity sprung into action, dual action, with fundamentalist staunchly opposing abortion and liberal elements supporting choice. Generally, the Black church remained silent on the subject for years. Some preachers reasoned it was better for Black women to get an abortion than to add yet another illegitimate child to the growing ranks spawned by the Sexual Revolution. This was a mistake.

Statistics now indicate Black women have a grossly disproportionate number of abortions to our population.[2] This tragedy is part the fault of the Black clergy for not defining abortion as our brothers across the aisle, and from adopting all the values of secular liberal humanism. This is how it became possible that full service Planned Parenthood is supported by Black clergy. Contraception's intended use for family became secondary in its use as a facilitator for degenerate sexual lifestyles, leaving abortion as the last ditch choice to maintain a woman's freedom. The latest technology, Plan B or the morning after pill, has been slated according to the manufacturer, to be marketed to the young women.[3] Where are the Black clergy on this issue? Celebrating with Planned Parenthood?

AIDS and STD's are testament to the epidemic of sexual immorality and adoption popular cultural norms counter to godly living. Evidently, it has been forgotten that the founder of Planned

Parenthood was a racist and proponent of Eugenics. This did not sway 400 pastors and Black religious leaders from supporting the "Keeping it Real" curriculum, joining voices in a humanistic response to problems stemming from sexual sins.[4] It seems to be easier to promote choice and condoms rather than preach biblical directives on sexuality. If the pastors were keeping it real, they would not ignore 1 Corinthians 6:9,18, Hebrews 13:4, and Revelations 21:8. The pitfalls of sexual impropriety and avarice are real enough for these preachers without needing to join hands with such an organization. The preachers' actions broadcast the message that real solutions are to be found at Planned Parenthood, not in the Gospel which is deemed impotent in the face of such a social problem.

For too long abortion has been presumed to be a White problem with Black clergy deferring their authority on the issue to pro-choice advocates. We have surrendered in the face of indisputable evidence that the Sexual Revolution and the welfare system are inferior to God-ordained parameters for sexual relations and family structure. Even social scientists have concluded the best environ for child rearing is the traditional husband/wife unit. Even that truth has been challenged as the Episcopal Church's ordination of an openly gay Bishop, Gene Robinson, has emboldened Gay activists to demand same sex marriage as a right that should be recognized as culturally legitimate.[5]

Now more than ever, the anti-family values that are being heralded as cultural options must be countered with scriptural imperatives buoyed by divine indicatives gleaned from our Savior. The secular humanists declare such changes are just part of modern living and; therefore, Christianity must change to keep current. As we can see from not only the American Episcopal Church but also from the Black clergy's actions and alliances, that they too believe the assumption. As the clergy holds to that presupposition, the powerful gospel of Jesus Christ is discounted as ineffectual rhetoric to the believer and unsaved alike; thereby, opening a door of doubt to be exploited by the Devil and the anti-Christ propaganda machine.

I was shocked one evening that a benefactor of God's dramatic action could be so bereft of faith in supernatural wisdom and power to solve worldly problems. Reverend Eugene Rivers of the Azusa Christian Community Church in Boston was the guest on National Public Radio's *The Connection* to discuss the numbing wave of Black on Black violence gripping South Central Los Angeles. Reverend Rivers is an activist minister and president of the Ten Point Coalition, a community-based group credited with reducing violence in the inner city of Boston. "Blessed be the peacemakers," Christ said on the mount, and we must applaud Reverend Rivers' work. Yet, I was startled when the radio host inquired: "What is the first thing you say to a hard case - do you tell them about God?" Reverend Rivers replied, in the most dismissive tone, that no experienced youth worker would ever give them a Sunday school lesson.[6] Since when is sharing the plan of salvation a Sunday school lesson? The power of the Gospel which has transformed the world, many nations, and countless lives is not enough to transform a local menace to society? This statement is yet another example of how far into humanist thought and away from faith in the power of Christ and God's Words has eroded basic elemental Christian beliefs among our ministers.

I have talked to numerous convicts who told me that as they grew up in the neighborhood, never once had a preacher so much as looked in their direction except with disdain. So many other "tough guys" seemed genuinely hurt by the experience. Are inner city pastors afraid of these youth? Is risk taking to share the gospel left only to Bible characters and figures in church history? Where is the faith to take not just another Government program to the streets but the redemptive news of the Cross first and foremost? There is a lack of faith, or rather, a faith that extends to the doors of the church. For those inside and outside the church house, the strongest indication of faith is exhibited in the pastoral use of gimmicks and marketing techniques to attract, retain, and grow the flock.

My wife and I decided to spend an evening at the movies. She chose *Chicago*, a movie adaptation of the Broadway musical. My favorite number was performed by the character Billy Finn, (Richard Gere), a flamboyant, efficacious trial lawyer. The song was called *Razzle-Dazzle*. As I later mused over the number, I was impressed with the thought; this secular show tune was a critique of the modern Black church.

Give 'em the old razzle dazzle

Razzle dazzle 'em

Give 'em an act with lots of flash in it

And the reaction will be passionate

Give 'em the old hocus pocus

Bead and feather 'em

How can they see with sequins in their eyes?

What if your hinges are all rusting?

What if in fact you're just disgusting

Razzle dazzle 'em

And they'll never catch wise![7]

Verse two's concluding notes imply that if the show is grand enough, they won't even notice one's ineffectiveness. Moreover, if the singing is lively, choir rocking the house, and the sermon style and substance is as equally complimentary, no one will question whether the pastor is really called.

Therein lies the question: Are you called? Does the fact that the Lord miraculously and graciously turned your individual life around mean that He called you to the pulpit to lead a flock? Is your authority genuine or assumed? Is it Jesus' choice that your son or daughter inherits the Church, or yours? Are you a female pastor because of Christ or the times? Behind the Sunday morning razzle-dazzle are you hopelessly ineffective and swamped by members requests for counseling and care? Do you really care for them? If the trustee board removed your name from the marquee and replaced it with Jesus' name (the true head of the Church), would you be offended or would you quit?

These are hard questions. The answers have enormous ramifications. The postmodern world has equipped the unbelievers and nominal believers alike with extraordinarily effective, hypocrisy sensitivity. This sensitivity does more to foster a cynicism that serves Satan's Kingdom as all Christian Orthodox truth is rejected with the uncovering of one false shepherd after another. So while the flock may not catch wise by your *Razzle-Dazzle*, how can you ignore the eyes that keep watch on the wicked and the good (Proverbs 15:3), and how will you be able to escape the words of the righteous Judge on the day of the Lord: "I never knew you. Away from me you evildoers (Matt.7:23)!"

Frankly, perhaps the problem is that you don't believe any of it. Maybe you are a secular humanist enjoying a religious career; you still cannot escape the insurmountable evidence of the condition of Black Americans. Either way your *Razzle-Dazzle* is part of the problem. Most people hate to be labeled, but it is necessary now to categorize Black clergymen:

Called active and effective

Called but distracted

Called but politically infatuated

Called but doctrinally distracted(due to world influences)

Called - burned out

Called but keeping up with the Joneses

Called but assisting church to keep up with the Joneses

Called but (fill in the blank)

Not called but apparently effective

Not called - orthodox

Not called - heretical

Not called - ineffective

Chances are many in those categories will be reticent to admit their condition. To do so one risks an intense, eternal wrath and judgment of God reserved for those who lead his children astray. Are you willing to chance partaking of the full cup of God's wrath? None of us can bear even a sip! Get off the Devil's mount of pride and renew your mind. Even though leadership has been historically denied to African American men, we have no right or license to sin and cover it up to protect our position. Leaders are humans, and humanity is prone to transgressions. When the pastor slips, he must quickly admit the wrong, and correct it setting the example for the congregation. Those who cover up sins by denying them or hiding them make themselves targets for blackmail (spiritual and natural). More importantly, they weaken the church with the "do as I say, not as I do" hypocrisy. Christ's representatives had better be sold on his message and true believers par none. They must be champions of holiness and lead by example. If you do not believe the Bible at face value and recognize you are to serve him and not be served, then consider leaving the pulpit. Do this for the sake of the community, your soul and Jesus Christ.

Pastor Marvin McMickle has recently called to Black ministers to alert the Black middle class of their responsibility to helping the underclass in his book, *Preaching to the Black Middle Class.*[8] yet McMickle's overemphasis on addressing racism overshadows his praiseworthy call to be our brother's keepers. The urgent need to address racism was relevant during the times of segregation and into the late 1970s. The racism African Americans encounter today is historically relatively mild and more often garden variety prejudice. When slights occur (real or imagined) our community typically blows the situation out of proportion. As the pluralism of America grows ever increasingly, we are experiencing an ideological challenge to our claims of existent debilitating racism by other ethnic groups. Asians, Latinos, Hawaiians, and others who have taken it on the chin for decades and are surging forward, represent a spoiler to our monolific claim of victimhood effects for every ill.

Pastoral overemphasis on racism ignores the biblical reality of sin's ever-presence. It will not be until the return of Christ that the earth will be purged of all sins, including racism. Racism is an evil that will be with us, furthermore, preachers are in a superior position to put racism's evil in proper context of the larger fallen world. McMickle missed an opportunity to identify the greatest problem confronting Black Christians of all economic stations: immorality and unholiness. McMickle's exhortation to the Black middle class to be the salt of the earth is admirable but does not go far enough.

Jonathan Edwards, universally recognized as one of America's greatest preachers, delivered a sermon titled "Sin and Wickedness Bring Calamity and Misery on a People" from Proverbs 14:34 which states, "Righteousness exalteth a nation: but sin is a reproach to any people." Edwards made this observation, "When a

113

man is getting worse he understands his own badness less and less."[9] Jonathan Edwards' 18th Century estimation sums up the moral condition in our day. Our ministers must address our sin first, and refrain from the legacy of presenting a lopsided gospel.

During the 1970s hippies and postmodernists, by use of humanistic reasoning, challenged the doctrine that God could be a dispenser of wrath and judgment as well as love. Since American Christianity had declared the government's Vietnam campaign righteous and was proved to be in error, counter cultural challenges to traditional orthodoxy gained plausibility as many questioned how God could be love and punish humans with hell. American Christianity flinched at the ideological challenge, and the fire and brimstone message was relegated to a back seat so as not to offend mainstream sensibilities. Messages informing and containing imagery of God's wrath were considered over the top.

Since that time masses of Americans have been shortchanged on the Gospel and the point of Christ's earthly ministry. How can Christ's actions be fully appreciated unless people understand just what they were saved from. Moreover, the "God is love" only message gives leave to believers to brush off biblical calls to holiness. The unmerited grace offered through Christ degenerates into a free pass to heaven with no strings attached. The Devil scored a coup as the traditional doctrine of heaven and hell was modified to fit cultural sensitivities.

Robert Peterson is the foremost Evangelical scholar on the traditional doctrine of hell. He contends in *Hell on Trial* that the absence of clear, biblically defined eternal destinies from Christian leaders has left believers susceptible to influence by the myriad of afterlife scenarios generated in a pluralistic culture.[10] Due to this, Christians supposedly privy to the ultimate truth are as confused as everyone else. The confusion has facilitated a window of encroachment for proponents peddling heretical doctrine deceiving the flocks.

As agents of God's truth, we must advance the complete doctrine to the world. The truth is, Jesus saves us from hell, a hell humanity deserves for its rebellion and sin. The God of the universe is truth personified. Compromised flesh cannot share the same space with Him who does not compromise. The world rejects the idea of a supreme authority. It declares the buck stops with men, and its wise men will challenge all who do not share this view unto death. Those are the facts and persecution is the cost that Christ's servants are called to partake. If anyone wants to compromise they had better stick to politics. We cannot. The condition of our communities bears witness to the cost. Our clergy owe the people the truth on exactly what the penalty is for brazen immorality. Once people understand from that which they are saved, love and gratitude for the risen Christ blossoms and grows. When emergency room nurses report gang members dying in the emergency room show no regrets or confess nothing as they leave this life, Black preachers must ask, "Are we of any use?" [11]

Dietrich Bonhoeffer posed that question to the clergy in Nazi Germany who failed to oppose and pronounce blessings on Hitler's fascist regime.[12] Are we of any use when Christ died for these misguided men and they were never informed of the fact? God wants the Crips saved as much as the Buppie. Both have value in God's eyes, and both will suffer the same fate unsaved. If Jesus had the most to say about heaven and hell during his ministry, shouldn't his representatives as well? Are the servants greater than the master? If they aren't at IBM or ATT, then how can they be in the Kingdom of God? The traditional doctrine of Hell is just one of a number of dominions left unchallenged by Black clergy.

Unchallenged Dominions

In November of 2003, I picked up Reverend Jesse Lee Peterson's *Scam.* Peterson, in his radio interviews and on the internet, touted *Scam* as the definitive book defining all that is wrong with Black America and its Left leaning leadership. As I finished it, I was disappointed as yet another prominent Black preacher elected political posturing for personal gain while denouncing similar action in others. Peterson's most striking statement, "Forty years ago Blacks were ashamed of sin," was lost in a milieu of standard issue Left bashing.[13] His simplistic view that conservative Republicans represent the Hezbollah (Party of God) of our day is as laughable as his characterizing all Democrats as "evil," "racist" and communist. Apparently, Peterson was unaware the Cold War had ended and we won.

Scam is yet another scam perpetrated by Black clergy more allegiant to the cult of the dollar than Jesus Christ. Our shepherds are too busy securing retirement accounts, chasing celebrity, engaging in commercial networking, and political grandstanding than seeing about the needs of a neglected and malnourished flock. Peterson's discourse in *Scam* was culturally accurate but lost in a tirade of political vulgarities. His reductionist view of American history generously under-dramatized monstrous historical wrongs and Christian involvement in typical fashion by those championing a political conservative worldview. It is astounding that Christians and Christian leaders who are supposed to be committed to truth, can neither accurately or honestly discuss American history while maintaining fundamentalist doctrinal views.

The current dual camp posture is an affront and stumbling block to those who should be primarily focused, if not obsessed, with sharing the Gospel. Which scriptural text laid down the foundation for the doctrine of political affiliation? Who does that serve? American Christianity is already divided by denomination and race. Political divisions are yet another handicap. Conservatives are very clear in their allegiance to the flag first, Christ second. Liberals are equally committed to humanistic supremacy and share a self-righteous strain with its opposite. Each side deifies its leaders, never truthfully discussing their failures as sinful fallen men. This bombastic posturing has corrupted the Black clergy. Pastors on each side avoid using the full lens of scripture to interpret culture; instead they lean into their own understanding using biblical passages to accessorize personal ideologies. Shepherds who can wrest themselves away from both camps and dare to stand independently in sole allegiance to Christ are best equipped to transmit an apolitical gospel with its transcendent message. Lost in the conflicting ideological debate is the scriptural truth that we Christians are strangers and aliens to this world (1 Peter 2:11). Our failure to sever the mooring to our national identity ill equips adherents to the faith to question whether the American dream's accruing of treasures on earth is Christ's dream for America.

Again, we must consider Bonhoeffer's challenge, "Are we of any use?" Are we of any use when our fixation on attendance roles and

118

political turf wars has field stripped the purpose and tenor of the sermon? Are we of any use when behind all the Left and Right positioning, few working solutions have been presented or implemented to address our litany of problems? Are we of any use as our people transition from historical victims to victimizers? Are we of any use as our art, politics and home life shout immorality rules, and in our outlandish vanity we obsessively search for a racist speck in our brother's eye? The Black clergy can again be of use by exerting the authority of scripture.

Gambling

Here in the Midwest where I live, there are five "riverboat" casinos in the St. Louis metropolitan area with plans for a sixth moving swiftly forward. Most have sumptuous buffets which I have been inclined to patronize. One evening as my wife and I waited to go into the casino's buffet, we decided to engage in anthropological exercise for fun (people watching). In our unscientific manner (counting heads) we observed an inordinate number of middle-aged Black women heading for the slots. Of those who passed us, one quarter were rushing as if they were guaranteed a payout. Others were dressed as if they just woke up, with two entering with curlers dangling from their hair! The fact that many are allured by the exaggerated sounds of slot machines paying out, the lights, and the over-hyped promises of action plastered

119

across countless billboards is not remarkable in itself. What is remarkable is that the St. Louis Metropolitan Clergy coalition (Black preachers) helped to surmount the opposition to legalized gambling.

Those opposing gambling forwarded two main arguments. The first was against gambling for moral reasons with its degenerate influence increasing a rainbow of potential ills. Their second assertion being negative economic impact. Armed with statistics from other communities, they disclosed that unless 90% of the casino patrons came from outside the area, the economic impact would be negative for the region.

Our Coalition of Christian Leaders touted that the casinos would mean more jobs and dollars desperately needed for education. Let me repeat, our clergy were promoting the merits of legalized gambling in terms of jobs. These same men were expected to be taken seriously on matters of the spiritual and on the path to truth, yet these same ministers would wager that the Black community would avoid further submersion in risky behavior and reap employment benefits from an exploitive industry.

The casino's smattering jobs held by Blacks proves to be crumbs compared to the tens of millions more dollars of inheritance, savings, and disposable income which floods the coffers of an industry that legitimized itself from its bloody organized crime origins. Even

120

old Al Capone would be proud as the masses accept an illegal game gone mainstream by the handiwork of marketers and not machine gunners. Gambling stands out as an unchallenged dominion unaddressed and under-addressed by those charged with the spiritual development of humanity.

Heresies and Witchcraft

Multiculturalism's peeling away of the White monolific influence on American culture and steering the country toward an inclusive respect for ethnicity has been one of the positive effects of postmodernism. Contributions to American history and culture neglected benignly and deliberately by Whites are now being made known and receiving new found appreciation as we collectively work to season to taste all ingredients in our national melting pot. The downside comes in the form of celebration and legitimization of pagan idolatry. Voodoo, Buddhism, Candomble, Islam, Santeria and Rastafarianism are now all declared as valid as the gospel of Jesus Christ. [14] The militantly concocted Kwanzaa receives equal legitimacy in the Christmas season. Psychics such as Miss Cleo and others pander to and are patronized by the same community claiming to be 81% Christian. Our adoption into God's family through the knowledge of Jesus Christ freed us from the bonds of witchcraft and ancestor worship common to Africa. Now these discarded shackles are characterized as a freedom denied to us by the slave system. As if the rising popularity and integration of the New Age occultic elements into popular culture weren't bad enough, now African Americans are told they should be angry the "freedom" to practice witchcraft was denied by Whites during slavery! We should be praising God that idolatry was suppressed and not returning to our own vomit.

Social critic Alan Wolfe recently proclaimed, "American culture has triumphed in the transformation of American religion," in his book of the same title.[15] That statement is easily observed in the domain of the Black church. The Black clergy have had to back away from scriptural absolutes in order to keep its liberal political bride happy. That bride, like Ahab's Jezebel, demands her religion of postmodern relativism must be worshiped in order to enjoy the fruits of Naboth's vineyard. Marital vows require the Black clergy and community to forever don the straightjacket of victimhood and nourish the children with a gruel of Christianity-lite. An ever-growing array of conditions and dominions go unchallenged by the Black preacher who is out of step with his historical role models. When issues are addressed such as AIDS, they are framed in non-scriptural context. These prescriptions and warnings are powerless and the people remain trapped in cycles of sin.

Pride

There exists a quiet smugness shared by Blacks in the mistaken belief that certain crimes or sins we just don't commit. For years Black leaders of all ilks have used these examples as a line to connect the dots to slavery in order to paint Whites as collectively more immoral than Blacks. Take the case of the D.C. Snipers. In the fall of 2002 when the snipers' reign of terror appeared to be ending, news outlets began to profile the now convicted John Muhammad. I watched a CBS evening news piece in which Blacks were publically saying, "Please don't let him be one of us." Are White snipers only acceptable? Our arrogance in being overly concerned with a collective image as ten families (Blacks included) grieved loss is appalling. Locally, in my hometown, a similar scenario played out to absurd extremes.

The St. Louis area turned out to be the crime scene for the midwest's most prolific Black serial killer to date, Maury Travis. On St. Louis Black talk radio, the theory was being circulated that Travis was being set-up as a serial killer to make us look bad. Travis' jailhouse suicide added gasoline to the conspiratorial flames. Later the police and news outlets revealed to the public videos of Travis in the midst of committing the sadistic crimes. Those claiming such conspiracies as a matter of protecting Black pride were made to be fools.

Further evidence of our prejudices can be uncovered in the most unusual places. During the September 17 airing of the deplorable Howard Stern Show, James Brown revealed that as BET honored him on their 2003 Annual Awards show for lifetime achievement as an entertainer, they refused to allow his wife on stage with him because she was White.[16] Brown stated they were not up front about it and led he and his wife to believe that she would perform on stage with him. How soon we forget. It is humanly impossible to calculate or tally all of the incidents by Whites when access was denied to us because of our color. If it was wrong for them, it is wrong for us. Why are we so comfortable in staking claims of which sins we do and don't commit? We denounce racism and prejudice at every turn, but the light skin versus dark skin drama still plays out despite wide collective knowledge of its divisive roots in slavery. And while the intention of this reverse pride may be a sociologically recognized survival mechanism common to oppressed peoples, it is still pride. This pride is sin, and it has been under-addressed from Black pulpits. The Apostle Paul clearly addressed the issue in Romans, as he informed his Jewish audience that they were not superior to the Gentile as they believed, but equally condemned with all humanity; all deserving God's righteous judgment for sin. The same goes for us, historically victimized or not. Without Christ we stand judged.

The whole prideful mindset has infected our people with a we-can-do-no-wrong attitude. John McWhorter argued in *Losing the Race* that this is a logical byproduct of a perpetual victim ideology. To that point I agree, and add this is a further mutation of the oppressed people's pride syndrome.[17] Whether couched in sociological terminology or otherwise, it is the basic maintenance of pride, the original sin. Just as Blacks have historically questioned the legitimacy of American Christianity which supported enslavement and oppression, we must question our Christianity as we covertly harbor a perception of moral superiority. Is the sum of our misery greater than other oppressed peoples? Do we definitely know that we've suffered more than the Chechens, the Palestinians, Armenians, South Africans or the Native Americans? Consequently, God's record book only reads as sins committed against Him. The Black clergy must collectively emphasize the doctrine of original sin to place sins committed against us and the ones we commit in proper perspective. Our clergy must challenge their members to identify and, as Jonathan Edwards would say, mortify that sin. The scalpel of scripture can only cut this cancer out of the Black collective body. Proverbs 16:18 states, "Pride comes before destruction, a haughty spirit before a fall." We have fallen, the word must go out so we can get up.

125

Pimps and Players

The 1970s Black exploitation film glorification of the pimp has not died out, but has been resurrected in its new form, the player. We have observed gangster rap heavyweight such as Nelly, Snoop Dog, Jay-Z, DMX , 50 Cent and an armada of like- minded proponents declaring the pimp legitimate. Since not everyone is cut out to be a pimp, you can aspire to be a player or "playa." What is a pimp? What purpose does he serve in society? None, other than his own. A pimp is a manipulator of the weak, a sexual exploiter of women and the epitome of predatory narcissism. While the United Nations Council on Human Rights works to denounce the sex trade and sexual exploitation in its New York Headquarters, the brothers passing by it on the street greet each other with "what's up playa," that is if they greet. The Black vernacular has always given birth to new hip terms that are now quickly adopted by Fifth Avenue marketers. The reintroduction and variations of the term pimp, i.e.: pimping, pimp slap, pimp juice, used by youth and the celebrity elite bestow legitimacy on behavior that is depravity defined.

Recently, a dear friend attended a workshop in Washington, DC for teenage girls rescued from prostitution. He said that after you've talked face to face with young women whose lives have been ravaged so some guy can get paid, you would recoil at the mere utterance of pimp. The pimp's ideological son, the player, is an exploiter of a lesser degree. His goal is to live off the backs of gainfully employed women. Cash, lodging and amenities are dispensed to him because of his sexual proficiency. The player, like the pimp, has many women to facilitate his high roller materialistic lifestyle. Both the pimp and the player are social pariahs. Both are routinely saluted in rap and R&B music hits. Ironically, the pimp is a perpetuation of the slave master model vociferously denounced in its historical form. And while the player's lifestyle spins off the pimp in a modestly subversive way, both exploit women and manipulate emotion for personal benefit. Each is representative denigration of work, another popular theme in hip hop music. Hard work or real work is left to the victim or suckers who would be so naïve as to follow societal norms. Young men and women are indoctrinated to envy and emulate the player's lifestyle seen in videos, heard in music, and reported by the news outlets affixation on celebrity as we discussed in Chapter 4.

Where are our clergy in opposition to this toxic proselytism? Shockingly, some clergy see it fit to emulate these pimps and players in style, dress and demeanor. Instead of modeling Paul's call to dress modestly, our look must reek of prosperity. Generations X and Y have observed the clergy keeping up with the Joneses and Jacksons and have decided to remain outside the church doors in an interest of "keeping it real". Of course no one is advocating pastors dress like paupers, but if the pimp is to be denounced from the pulpit, the reverend had better not look like one.

We must be vigilant to analyze and critique any new lifestyle that is introduced into the culture. The men of God should condemn what must be condemned, even the supporting language. Words are powerful. Words start wars, arguments, religions, relationships and, as we know from the Bible, start life. The common usage of terms such as pimp and players serve to glorify and validate those characters. How dare we glorify monsters, legitimize wickedness and crown degeneracy as authentic Black culture. The Black church has failed to keep up with cultural changes.

The Church is instructed to be as wise as the serpent and as gentle as doves (Matthew 10:16). This is necessary for Christians as we use the light to expose the enemies' schemes to the world, drawing the unsaved to the source of protection and salvation. In Luke 6:39 Jesus used the illustration with a question, "Can a blind man lead the blind?" Can the church lead people blinded by the world if it is blind to the way the world works?

Unfortunately, the Black church is not alone in its need to catch up. American Christianity trails behind American culture, especially in addressing possible outcomes with the too fast and too furious introductions of new technologies. Pastors should have been able to foresee that instant and text messaging would attribute to and increase female bullying. The clergy should be on point with biblical perspectives concerning new cultural inventions in order to stay relevant. If the church is leading the path to enlightenment, pastors will not need to worry about implementing strategies and models for church growth.

Money Theology

Too often preachers remark that if one loses his or her job, the Lord has a better job waiting for you. That mantra is presumptively arrogant. The person may or may not get a better job. Should the person ignore the offers of lesser paying jobs and march into financial arrears in waiting for that better job? No, God promises to provide for our needs, spiritually, first, and physically, second. The Israelites were fed daily with manna and their clothes did not wear out during the 40 years wandering in the desert. God did not rain filet mignon down from the heavens, nor did new designer clothes miraculously appear on their backs because they were God's people. He simply met their needs.

Now let us consider the latest heresy: the prosperity message. Daily TBN and others pump via satellite around the world an American mutation of Christianity. Its message is that the signs of a successful Christian are financial prosperity: don't have enough money, well pray the prayer of Jabez. If the financial blessings aren't flowing in, then question your level of faith. This bogus call to materialism has camouflaged itself as trappings of the Gospel.

It is interesting that few preach Paul's exhortation to be content within Jesus, broke or loaded (Philippians 4:11). To be content in America is to be at a logger's head with the consumer culture's ideology: financial and material dissatisfaction (covetousness). Shared American dogma requires the citizenry to work tirelessly until the dream of home ownership, complete with white picket fence and retirement account, is realized. Furthermore, while promises of freedom have drawn multitudes to these shores, so has the prospect of becoming rich. The same dream concocted by humans is masqueraded as part of the way to salvation. Christ's righteous work extended freely to man to justify humanity is now utilized as a stage prop in a global marketing presentation. May God have mercy on us for allowing this disrespectful heretical message to go forth unchallenged. The reason for its existence is more evidence of the clergy's adulterous ongoing relations with money. To be honest, American New Testament teachings on money clash with the reality of overflowing abundance. Popular culture heralds the rich for their success, and despite some minor cosmetic differences, economic orientations are readily apparent in our "classless" society. From public policy (Left and Right); the media; and daily life we can see, as James Gilligan argued in *Violence*, that the poor are made to feel ashamed of their station.[18] Cynically, preachers have recited Jesus' statement of the poor always being among us (Matthew 26:11) as a green light to ignore their plight. So how convenient it is to tie evidence of ones faith to economic viability. Consider the consequences as this corrosive message reaches a new convert in a township in South Africa he is thrown into a quandary because the riches promised by the American televangelist do not materialize for him, his family, and his town. Dare we place stumbling blocks to those bought and paid for with the precious blood of Jesus? Dare we earn the woes our savior lodged at the Pharisees for the mishandling of converts (Matthew 23:13-15)? We must quickly remove such obstacles. This warped corruption of the Gospel must end.

Dick Gregory once likened Black pastors' ability to raise funds with being able to get blood from a turnip. So often the call to give denigrates to the level of sales pitch. You've heard the time tested, "You can't out-give God by line," or the call to give with the expectation of the coming blessing. This and other claims are psychological orchestrations that precede offertory regimen. The tithe box is placed forward for all to see who the real "Christians" are. This perspective is fundamentally flawed.

The Devil's chief charge lodged against Job was that his Godly obedience was solely due to receipt of physical blessings. The scriptures show us quite the opposite and we learn about the greatness of God, his sovereignty, and the proper attitude to take as we suffer trials. Most importantly, we learn that the material props that dot our walk as servants to God are of no importance to Him nor are they to be used as a divine favor indicator.

If the message goes out to expect more if something is taken away, or expect a blessing when we give, then the Christian walk is rendered a bartering faith. In that since we still are at a cosmic disadvantage because you can't out give God, who has given all through Jesus Christ. Our posture towards giving should be out of respect to our Sovereign God and provider, out of love to our Lord, and with no expectation other than God's promise to provide. Christ said "store up for yourselves treasures in heaven", (Matthew 6: 20a). There they are safe because God handles the security and bookkeeping. Only a lack of faith in words of our savior or a deliberate choice to feed the sheep a fast food Christian message can account for the existence continuation and dissemination of such propaganda.

Greed

We have already touched upon the failures of pastors to preach contentment to their congregations. As contentment is antithetical to our consumer driver economy, ads and commercials have indoctrinated us so effectively that few Christians realize that they are immersed in convetousness. The desire for more things fuels the desire or the love for the means to acquire those precious things. Show us the money. It is the love of money that has been the root of infamous historic American evils. Today this love undermines most aspects of American culture. Let us start with Education.

Contemporary conventional wisdom has described college as no more than a means to a prosperous end; therefore, whatever methods used to get to college are fair game. Cheating is rampant and widespread in high schools and college. Some parents opt having their children labeled ADD in order to secure more testing time for SAT/ACT tests. Colleges assist students in ruining their credit by permitting credit card companies to hook students for access fees. Collegiate athletic programs are so addicted to bountiful revenues they fail to educate the Black participants.[19] School districts hungering for revenues have co-opted concerns for children's health in allowing Coke and Pepsi to peddle junk food to youth already bombarded by marketers beckoning to unhealthy eats.

The world of education is just the tip of the iceberg. For fear of sounding like a Marxist diatribe, I will curtail expounding on this point. It is a blessing to live in a land of prosperity and conversely a curse. The average American believer and non-believer can quickly and easily be seduced into a love affair with money. We have discussed money theology and its errors, but as American clergy we must be aggressive, vocal and persistent in warning against greed.

Missions

It is curious that Black Americans have widely and pridefully accepted the sobriquet African American despite its inaccuracy. African-Americans, including Black Muslims, exhibit little interest in Africa and African affairs, especially since the ending of Apartheid. Africans and Africans in America will confirm that point readily. Even African American Christians have long neglected to share the gospel on the African Continent and just about everywhere else. For all the ongoing criticisms of White Christianity, one cannot ignore their faithfulness to the call to evangelize the world. Black clergy, in an interest of retaining power and resources, have stifled Black missionary work levels of statistical insignificance.[20]

Marvin McMickle recently documented great Black American Christian figures in his *Encyclopedia of African American Christian*

Heritage. From the very beginnings of the Black church in America, mission work was heavy on the minds of pioneering Black ministers. Carey Lott zealously decried, "I long to preach to the poor Africans the way of life and salvation", and he did in 1821.[21] Other men such as Daniel Coker, George Liele and Peter Williams, Jr. aggressively and fearlessly answered Christ's (Acts 1:8) call. Today, international mission work is vigorously pursued by White Christians. Apart from the February donning of kinte cloths and the surname, African Americans are not interested in sharing the gospel with their African brothers. Worse yet, the idea that monetary resources would divert out of the community parish is unthinkable to some pastors. Prominent pastor and author, Marvin McMickle, omitted the subject in *Preaching to the Black Middle Class*. The Black middle class growing in wealth and prosperity are the most able to forage into international missions, but McMickle holds to the line in declaring racism as Black pastoral priority. The Black church's record on missions is yet another sign that even the basic gospel is not being disseminated or heeded.

Women as Pastors

July 11, 2000 was heralded as a great day for the African Methodist Episcopal Church (AME) as they elected their first female bishop, Vashti McKenzie. McKenzie, herself seminary trained, declared triumphantly, "The stained glass ceiling has been broken."[22]

135

While breaking the glass ceiling is and was necessary to all society outside the church, scripture is clear that it is not what God intended for the church. Many churches in America have been holding closely with societal trends, tramping upon the authority of scripture along the way. McKenzie and many other women have been installed as overseers, bishops and deacons, despite clear scriptural criteria for those offices.

I have read the impassioned testimonies of many regarding their call to preach and heard some of their capable preaching, but does efficacy assure calling? Has any woman who stepped into the shoes of pastorship ever asked God why He would call her to do something contrary to His revealed truth in scripture? Has tracking with the world ever been an appropriate barometer for testing actions within the church? How can any woman call others to believe in the inerrancy of God's Word when they ignore scriptures themselves? The Word is currency of God's sovereignty. Just as counterfeiters harm our economy, biblical counterfeiters damage the economy of the church. Christ's free currency suffers deflation and rejection as "Christians" print up amended bills to reflect the nature of the market. Unlike Alan Greenspan, the Divine Board chairman has changed nothing to His graceful stimulus package.

Women have great freedom and more work available than is acknowledged to do in the church. If Black women were operating at their fullest as evangelists, prophets, teachers and healers, we would not be drowning in a tsunami of immorality. As it stands, our women are as depraved and distracted as our men. Scripture declares leadership of the church is left to men. Is God's sovereignty at question? Advocates against it are in error. The historical precedent for women as ordained pastors and bishops has opened the door for an openly gay Episcopal bishop, Gene Robinson, to be installed. Robinson is where he should be if scripture is not to be viewed as inerrant and is required to be diluted with the historical critical lens. In that case why shouldn't women, the openly gay, and why not children be ordained as bishops, deacons and elders.

If you look past my sarcasm you will find consistency in a logical deductive pattern of arguing. We must remember the wisdom of the world, may work for the world but it is foolishness in God's sight. His foolishness makes more sense than we can understand in this body. If we believe in Him, in the resurrected son, and His word we must live it despite current cultural trends.

137

The Down Low

I have saved what I believe is one of the most threatening trends for final discussion of unchallenged dominions. Recent reports have leaked out of mainstream media outlets about the Down Low lifestyle.[23] As HIV infection and the AIDS mortality rate skyrockets among Black women, information about the Down Low lifestyle has emerged. Increasing numbers of Black men are exploring bisexuality and engaging in illicit sex with gay men. These men are then returning home to their wives, lovers, and cohabitating partners infecting them with HIV. These men hide their actions and cover their tracks by appearing virulently anti-gay.

Some of the Black activists, now publicly revealing the lifestyle, have blamed the behavior on the Black community's "homophobia." This is the reasoning publicly expressed by those righteously "exposing their risky lifestyle." Apparently, we are to sit back quietly and permit these monstrously depraved men to sentence Black women to suffering, bankruptcy, and death, as well as orphaned lives to their children, for fear of being branded homophobic. These participants of the Down Low lifestyle must be condemned and castigated as fiends, enemies of Black people and humanity in general. Preachers should use this aberrant behavior as an opportunity to reacquaint the saved and unsaved with God's prescribed penalty for wickedness and immorality. As we can see in the absence of a clear and vocalized doctrine of hell, our community of believers has no fear as they parcel out hell on earth in pursuit of sexual gratification. These spineless, gutless cowards would rather the world collapse around them than have their pride bruised by accurate name-calling and public looks of disapproval. Some behaviors rightly earn communal disdain, and this is one of them. Even victims of some of the vilest murders are not subjected to the long term suffering the practitioners of the Down Low lifestyle casually and callously mete out. Pastors need to lay down the law and the love. Jesus can, will and wants to forgive those living the Down Low lifestyle and a myriad of others. If a denunciation of the Down Low lifestyle is taken as a swipe at the gay/bisexual/transgendered community, then so be it. The Gospel will offend, but to righteous ends.

Church as Lifestyle

Today in American society the rugged hoary individualism has been cast into terms of lifestyle. In the U.S. you are free to live the lifestyle you choose. The relativism doctrine provides on supportive ideology. There are many lifestyles to choose from. As I visited a boat and RV show, I found out there is an RV lifestyle. There is the gay lifestyle, the extreme lifestyle for the young, and in keeping with the times, the Black church offers the church lifestyle.

An individual can come get his shout on and practice a no-strings-attached spirituality. The Sunday worship service will rival most performances of the previous night in the club district with volume and concocted emotion. The best numbers are reserved for the offertory period because even nightclubs have a cover charge - you cannot expect to be entertained like that for free. One must bear with additional calls for special offerings and back tithes. If Whitney Houston can charge fifty dollars for a concert ticket, then the church deserves at least twenty for its performance.

The Black church lifestyle is comfortable for members. The pastor paints Jesus as the great problem solver or bail bondsman the members can call on when in trouble. Little else is demanded except regular tithing. The member is securely connected with popular culture as they are afforded close proximity to a celebrity figure, the pastor. The pastor/celebrity enjoys the best seats at the table, is well dressed and well fed. His or her name is plastered everywhere so the members will not forget it whenever they utter, "My pastor ___." The pastor's celebrity status is affirmed by political visits during election time, and the pastor is so gracious he doesn't expect the visiting VIP to sit through the sermon. He does expect raucous verbal affirmation of the subject (regardless of its exegetical nature). Once a year during the pastor's appreciation day or on his birthday, intense adoration (verbal and fiscal) is expected.

Now many may be offended by the characterization of the Black church as an alternative competing lifestyle. Unless it and those who lead it return to fundamental adherence to scripture, the church will be nothing more than a lifestyle as powerless and inconsequential as the medieval Catholic Church. We will discuss the future in the next chapter.

Rodrick Burton

Chapter 10

END GAME

The major threat to Blacks in America has not been oppression, but rather the loss of hope and absence of meaning. –Cornel West

Restore to me the joy of your salvation and grant me a willing spirit to sustain me. –Psalm 51:12

While it is always seemingly easier to recognize and diagnose problems, the solving portion is always the greatest challenge. Our world is complex and everyone from politicians to sociologists offer solutions devoid of attempts to address root causes. Fortunately, for Bible-believing Christians the answers are simple. It is when we insist on viewing the world through the human-centered lenses that the view becomes obfuscated and dark. The Bible tells us that sin and the fall of man is the root of our misery, and while there may be no comfort in that knowledge, we can be comforted that God has secured not only a way out of this mess, but the comforting power to live in the here and now. Our God and our Messiah are grieved when we who claim His name look away as Peter did focusing on the troubling waters. It was not until Peter cried out, "Lord save me," that Jesus reached out and saved him from drowning (Matthew 14:29). We are drowning in a tumultuous sea of immorality, and instead of looking to the same hand that rescued us from a lengthy history of natural oppression we look elsewhere. We have convinced ourselves that we can tread water forever or swim to shore one thousand miles away on our own. This is much like the popular fiction of pulling oneself up by his bootstraps. Invariably, in every such tale there is always someone or some situation unacknowledged as the true reason for the success. God is shortchanged for the supposed indomitability of the human spirit, just as with the case of the Civil Rights victory. It was not Martin Luther King, Jr. alone, but thousands working for justice with the true impetus for success coming from God's desire for justice. He saved us with the sacrifice of his son and it was an infusion of Christ love flowing from oppressed hearts that melted the hardest opposition rooted within the psyche of those claiming the same faith.

We need that kind of power to save Black Americans from an unraveling taking place at our natural core - the family, and eroding our inner core - our spirituality. As we continue to fail our Savior with our ignorance of scripture and subsequent disobedience to it, will our pastors and teachers secure their obsolescence by reinterpreting God's Word to fit the times? There will be two paths

144

blazed from this juncture: redemption and restoration from on our faces; or continued disgrace, earthly judgment followed by eternal damnation. For those who believe this is all fear mongering please reread chapter threeand continue on.

Disease (HIV/AIDS) and criminal violence continue to lead death's charge through the Black populace. Despite mountains of accurate information and an unprecedented compilation of delivery means, Blacks are catching and swiftly dying from a preventable illness. Yes, as the Ugandans have demonstrated, abstinence prevents HIV and AIDS infection as well as abstaining from intravenous drug use.[1] What is not mentioned is the threat of a new emerging virus incubating within the mounting ranks of the incarcerated: Hepatitis C.

Apart from those on death row or serving life without parole sentences, 90% of those in prison will be released. In addition to prisoners released with HIV/AIDS and TB, now and thousands more in the future will return to Black communities infected for life with a disease that can be transmitted through not only the standard HIV routes, but even a bloody fist fight. The shamefully small amount of medical attention delivered by a few HMO's, society's scornful indifference to the criminally convicted, and the media's self-censorship account for this newest health threat.[2] Since we have proportionately the greatest number of prisoners in the penal system, we will suffer the greatest ravages of this coming epidemic. To compound this problem, fiscal belts continue to tighten to support political and national objectives (War on Terror and tax cuts). Social programs will be cut. Moneyed special and corporate interest will continue to guide and influence policy interspersed with an occasional non-substantial nod toward Black Americans. Funds for medical resources to treat our non-voting, non-contributing, second ranking ethnic block will be scarce. Furthermore, we must expect that un-evangelized, under-employed, and scorned ex-convicts will have no communal sense of inclusion to prohibit behavior conducive to Hepatitis C's widespread transmission.

We must also consider the possibility of what I term as a Rwandan Syndrome. Left unchecked, as our traditional family base shrinks and a larger percentage of Black children are raised in single parent families going on to participate in the smorgasboard of risky behaviors, with many leading down the road of criminality, a Black criminal class will continue to grow. The convicted, unemployed, disenfranchised male population, in the absence of a meaningful, message is disposed to receive an alternative message.[3] A pied piper speaking in the code of rap and sporting a Five-percenter ideology has the potential to woo many. If these masses are then taught to no longer hate Whites, but instead blame those who left the ghetto behind for integration and prosperity without substantively "giving something back." A call to make the Black middle class pay for the underclass' suffering could lead to internecine culling unlike anything America has ever seen. This would be class warfare taken to a literal level. Apart from the body count, the negative effects on Black Americans would be manifold. A crime wave on such a scale would overwhelm the court system, meaning a possible imposition of martial law. Martial law would mean a disruption in economic activity, and in that absence, most Americans would unite in the disdain of Black Americans. We would understand the meaning of the Lord exposing our nakedness to the nations for all to see (Nahum 3:5-7).

Before discounting the possibility of such an event transpiring, one must consider what happened in Rwanda. Throughout its colonial period, the Belgians favored the Tutsi ethnic group. Despite being liberated since 1959, the acrimonious tension between the two groups lay beneath the surface as the prejudicial social regime continued. In 1994 when Rwanda's Hutu President, Juvenal Habyarimana, died in a mysterious plane crash, the call went out via radio to all Hutus to extract revenge on all Tutsis. One-hundred days and 800,000 bodies later the killing ended. Can such a thing happen here? Would those who sociologist, William Julius Wilson, described as "suffering intense hopeless forms of poverty," stop acting out on one another and launch a retributive campaign of Black on Black genocide? If the majority of killing in Rwanda were done with machetes, how would the proliferation of weapons on our streets affect the ensuing carnage?

To the unsaved and those unfamiliar with God's historical record presented in scripture, these nightmarish predictions would appear to be exercise in fanciful scare mongering. But to those who are familiar with God's Word know that He corrects those He loves and eliminates his enemies. The God of the Old Testament is the same as in the New. We must wonder then, how long will He tolerate those claiming to be His Son's representatives, the Son He sacrificed, to attempt to discredit that righteous work by their unfaithfulness and compromises with worldly values? Will God fail to correct his children and shepherds? Can we expect false teachers to get off the hook for leading humanity astray? Not without ignoring the Apostle Peter's shuddersome warning in 2 Peter 2. How long do we expect God to allow our condemnation of American Christianity's hypocrisy as we ignore our own?

Praise God for his exceedingly, incomprehensive mercy. Christ is waiting right now with hand extended for our collective repentance. God is incessantly worried about our fatherless and widows as he views 70% of the Black children born into that state. He knows multitudes of the mothers will live their lives as widows. He is concerned. Jesus wants to stand in the midst of wedding ceremonies and waits to pour out the wine of the Holy Spirit into the cups of those who would be faithful to Him and God's Word. God wants to restore us because He loves us. Our Savior loves us. Its time we turn to Him.

The remainder of this book is comprised of solutions, the first being to repent collectively. The solutions presented in this chapter are a blueprint, but we cannot forget what happened to Joshua and the Israelites. They believed they were capable of making the right decision and were tricked by the Gibeonites because they "did not inquire of the Lord" (Joshua 9:14). Our problems are immense and we do not know how to solve them. Therefore, after we repent we must ask for divine guidance and clarity for direction.

Solutions

The first step toward restoration with God is and has always been repentance. Some might ask, what are we repenting for? We have been the victims for centuries. Yes, that is true, but in recent years we have embraced that history and constructed an idol of it. This has produced a spirit of bitterness and spite with thankfulness being a scarce commodity. Our leaders posture our history as a tool to extract concessions and produce a spirit of superiority - yes, superiority, I'm better than you...look what you did to me. We would have never done that to you. That assumption is the height of human nature's ignorance.

All humanity is depraved. The victims today could be the human rights' violators of tomorrow. The blight of sin taints all groups. Yet, as sinners forgiven we must forgive. Is the servant greater than the master?

We must repent to White America for not acknowledging those who fought the good fights for justice; for painting so many with the brush of collective blame; for criticizing them for not reaching out to us; for extracting concession in a spirit of arrogance every chance we get; and for not setting the example of being the peacemaker, not for survival's sake but for love. The love that was extended to us by our Savior is to be shown to the greatest offender, and especially to our brothers. White Christians are our brothers. No student of the Bible needed science to verify the myth of race as the DNA that runs through us with our White brothers. We must pray this prayer:

Heavenly Father, creator of all humanity, we thank you for removing the barrier between us and you through your Son, our Savior, Jesus Christ. Such grace was unmerited on our behalf. Forgive us for not modeling such grace, forgive us for our intransigence. Forgive us for our erecting an idol of victimhood. Forgive us for not forgiving our enemies and brothers. Please allow the Holy Spirit to empower us to be the peacemakers and finish the work here in America started by Martin Luther King, Jr. Let the power of Christ be evident to the world as two groups with a bitter history unite in love and in a joint declaration of the gospel's power. What cannot be completed at this time, we look forward to its finalization under Christ's rule at His return. This we pray in the name of our glorified Savior, Jesus Christ. Amen.

This prayer is incomplete and less than perfect, but we owe such an apology to our God and fellow man.

In our anger and disappointment about the government not making a collective apology for slavery, two have been overlooked. In the appendix I have included apologies by two major Christian denominations, the Southern Baptist Convention and the Presbyterian Church of America. Neither in 1995 when the Southern Baptist's issued their apology, nor in the year 2000 with the PCA, did the press pay much attention. These unacknowledged apologies for slavery, while overdue, must be acknowledged and made known throughout the Black churches and communities. The expectation of a similar governmental decree is a naive fantasy, for we live in a land and time of tortmongering. This brings us to the subject of reparations.

As an act of contrition and thankfulness for all God has done for us, we Black Christians must put the reparation subject to rest. This will be the public sign that we forgive America, as her debt is pardoned as Christ pardoned ours. The idea of reparations at this historical juncture is comical. America is in the midst of its "War on Terror", which by all accounts will last for a considerable amount of time. Our healthcare costs are skyrocketing more each year. Sooner or later some administration will have to address that issue, which will be costly. Social Security solvency looms in the future as an enormous demographic transition to retirement. Americans expect our government to solve these fiscal behemoths, and we expect it to bankrupt itself on 12.7% of the population's claim for reparations? African-Americans need to "get real".

These are the points reparations proponents fail to address:

a) It is impossible to accurately estimate a figure of the total lost, denied and stolen wages for work during slavery and the Jim Crow era.

b) Even if such a total were calculated, the attempt to pay the enormous amount   would shatter the economy. No country in world history has bankrupted itself to pay restitution to an aggrieved minority.

c) The Black underclass would be ripped off again as affluent proponents declare the funds to be used for scholarships. Such scholarships would benefit the middle and upper class whose children are already in a fair position to take advantage of the rainbow of scholarships available now. Few have advocated using the reparations for job creation for the 24% Blacks living in poverty and for the incarcerated/ex-convicts.

d) Discussion about a violent backlash has been nonexistent. Racist organizations would have a rallying cry, and would enjoy the opportunity to advance from the fringes in the mainstream by challenging reparations payouts. A brief listen to Right-wing talk radio reveals a simmering resentment for Blacks being afforded equal access to welfare. Reparations would surely bring ideological support for the racial holy war pined by neo-Nazi's, the Klan, and like-minded militia groups.

All things considered, the reparations issue must be dropped. This should be done for Christ and in the interest of common sense. Every minute a pastor spends advocating reparations is time that should be spent advocating the Great Reparator. Dropping the reparations discussion lies on the road to restoration and is tied to our corporate repentance.

We must also ask forgiveness of the Black underclass who, as segregation ended were left behind as the Civil Rights victory opened new opportunities for the middle and upper classes. The underclass has been exploited by the Black political leadership to extract concessions from a society stricken with what Shelby Steele termed, "White guilt."

The concessions largely have benefited the Black middle class. The underclass has suffered scorn and condemnation for its visible sins while the middle and upper classes were able to keep them in the closet. They are no longer hidden. We must repent for that in-house hypocrisy as well. The next step following our confession would be to institute an Urban/Suburban fellowship.

Set up on the lines of the Big Brother, Big Sister program, a family or member of a prosperous congregation would be assigned through a local church a family or an individual in a distressed area. Fellowship, support, and an informational exchange would bring back the sense of community indicative of the pre-Civil Rights days. Information and exposure to life beyond the "hood" would spurn change in areas written off by society.

Immediately following our collective call for forgiveness, there must be a nationwide interdenominational evangelism drive focusing on college campuses, crime plagued areas, and among school-aged children.

One day while I was working with an elder in my church, he recounted a fond childhood memory involving Bible Baseball. Since I had never heard of Bible Baseball, my interest was piqued. During the 1950s, Methodists in the Louisville, Kentucky area would go to neighborhoods and set up a tent for Sunday School kids. They would serve refreshments, have a song, devotion, do a quick lesson (we are talking about kids) and wrap it up with a game of Bible Baseball. A batter could request a single, double, triple play or home run question. The kids would be organized into teams, usually boys versus the girls. The team with the highest score would win a prize - candy or novelty. At first the kids failed miserably, but by the second or third Sunday, the kids would have studied and excelled at a rapid pace and their familiarity with the Bible and Bible stories increased. I was awestruck and overjoyed at the method and the results. Therefore, as part of these plans for repentance, restoration, and revival of the Black family and church, I had to include this proposal: the M.S.M.U. (Mobile Sunday School Ministry Unit).

Just like the mobile mammogram units or library bookmobile, churches can rent an RV, bus, truck or whatever, set-up in an area on a glorious Saturday or Sunday afternoon in neighborhoods full of children, cutting across socioeconomic lines (naturally the more distressed areas would be first), and serve refreshments, teach them a song, have a quick to the point sermon, and wrap it up with a contest such as Bible Baseball, or Bible Basketball. This would follow a preliminary selection of a central site distribution of fliers and being prepared with follow-up programs to direct the kids to the MSMU. It should be around four week blocks, once in the spring and once in the summer before they return to school. The fourth week could be the grand contest week of Bible Baseball/Basketball with great prizes. All participants would get a free age-appropriate Bible. Just as on the foreign mission field, denominational affixation on turf control should yield to the greater cause of winning these young souls to Jesus. The college evangelism groups could follow the Campus Crusade model.

In Chapter 7, we discussed the church's mandate for addressing the needs of our incarcerated and convict populations. Evangelism in the streets should be spearheaded by ex-offenders working side by side with pastors, deacons and elders who are required by Christ to step outside their comfort zone to witness. Prison ministries must spawn a fully integrated approach, meaning that upon release the church must surround the former inmate with love and new influences as well as finding gainful employment for the individual. The employment dilemma is one of the most serious conundrums facing Black Americans. Prisoners are not only affected by transgressions against the state, but since September 11th, companies like ChoicePoint are being utilized by increasing ranks of employers, financial institutions, insurers, police and health providers to identify criminal, fraudulent, or problematic episodes in a person's history. Our society is gravitating towards a zero tolerance for any lapse in judgment; companies such as ChoicePoint are thriving from of retaining that history for all who pay to see. Honor and integrity have to be ingrained in the youth and minds of our people. While God, is as the Koran says, all merciful and oft forgiving, our society saves its forgiveness only for celebrity. The common man had better not make a mistake. In light of these realities, it should be the church leading the call to solve this underemployment problem with prayer, advocacy, and employment where possible.

In conjunction with the national evangelism campaign, our clergy must loudly and demonstratively preach against sexual immorality, promote marriage, and preach the traditional doctrine of hell. The Church must retrain the Black community to respect the authorities and to demand law and order in our homes and communities. Romans 13 is explicit in commanding Christians to obey the law and submit to the governing authorities. However, today we are ungovernable as we challenge police on every incident even as lawlessness elements run wild on the streets. Black leaders claim this scrutiny is necessary because the police can not be trusted due to brutality. Of course, we must address injustice aggressively; however, where is the justice for people who want to live in peace? The authorities are sanctioned by God to use force when necessary to subdue community rebels who repudiate the law and seek to live outside it by preying on the defenseless. Police forces are more professional today, reflective of the community, and attempting to be more culturally sensitive. This is a dramatic change from forty years ago. Will knuck-dusters, racists, and cowboy cops be on police forces? Undoubtedly. The police are still the police. We are to recognize them.

Our pastors should have a national week of rededication. In a solemn service started with prayer, every congregation would rededicate our sanctuaries with a sacred vow to the exclusive service to Jesus Christ. We must promise the Lord that His house will be a house of prayer; not a house of politics, not a house of cards, not a house of style, nor a house of pancakes. If the clergy don't respect the temple, how can we expect the community to respect it?

A consortium of pastors should start a special ministry dedicated to evangelizing, serving, mentoring and molding Black athletes and celebrities into strong Christian role models for the nation. Our clergy must work harder to recognize and understand cultural trends so that we can enable the flocks to use scripture to identify and avoid camouflaged snares. People outside the church will be drawn by discernment and wisdom exhibited by members. Wisdom is a scarce commodity in American life. We are drowning in technical knowledge, but there exists a dearth of wisdom.

International missions have long been neglected by the Black Church. An international outreach can coincide with the local one. African Americans must reach out to Africans, Asians, to our Latino brothers, the Europeans and wherever else the Lord directs.

Finally, we must prepare the flock to embrace the multiracial dimension of our faith as we have assumed ourselves to be unprejudiced; and yet as our society transitions away from the predominately White/Black perspective, we cannot don the "us versus them" worldview while declaring salvation's universal appeal. Simply put, we must learn from American Christianity's mistakes and not repeat them.

Back in July, I happened to catch an episode of *60 Minutes* that was transcendent. Peter Holsten, a Chicago real estate developer, tore down the infamous Cabrini-Green housing project and erected half a million dollar townhouses in its place.[4] Former Cabrini-Green residents were invited to live for free in the same luxury quarters selling for $500,000. Those purchasing homes were well aware and pleased that their neighbors would be former housing project residents. Holsten met with the Cabrini-Green residents to announce the opportunity to move out of the violent, cramped, and rundown quarters to all. He was met with anger, disbelief and rejection. A number hurled profanities at Holsten and City of Chicago officials. The program focused on those who stayed the course, followed the rules and guidelines, and who ended up neighbors with Chicago's upper-middle class. I thought this show was a parable about heaven. C.S. Lewis' *The Great Divorce* played out for anyone watching CBS on that July night.

The Black preacher has been condemned since slavery days for excessive emphasis on heaven. The criticism ratcheted up during the turbulence and remained high through those postmodern years. Many have backed away in response. This must revert to the way things were. When Jesus came to earth, His ministry focused on getting people ready for heaven and connecting them to it through sacrificing Himself. We are mortals and death is certain. In death we are unified with all humanity, either to rejoice through eternity with Christ or to suffer disgrace forever.

Heaven will not be segregated by race. So let's prepare the people for that and in a world full of questions, it is time that we honor Christ by providing the answers. Our people need answers, answers to questions not asked. This is the nature of the gospel. Comfort and peace lie in those answers provided in love by Jesus Christ. God has all the answers, such as how do we get back to Him. Nearly all have been provided in His precious words.

We stand on the verge of a great triumph in American Christianity as the world will bear witness to the improved moral state of Black America through the collective submission and faith in Jesus Christ.

ABOUT THE MESSENGER

Naturally, the communal reflex action is to declare these observations coupled with statistics as another attempt by some nobody to garner favor, finance, and fame in conservative circles. That assumption couldn't be further from the truth. While compiling data for this book there were a number of occasions in which the author could do nothing more than weep as the gravity of our situation pulled on my soul. So many times I considered quitting or throwing up my hands in a defeatist resignation. No one will listen was my prevailing common thought, especially since I considered myself to be a poor candidate to deliver any moral assessment due the fact my sins once contributed to crime and incarceration statistics.

Only when I considered the lives and words of the lesser prophets and Christ's worthiness of our service was I able to move on. Really, do you think Amos, Habakuk, and others were excited about pointing out the flaws in their people or pronouncing God's judgment on them? Only a sadist would revel in the pronouncement of bad tidings for his people. This book is a lament and an appeal for immediate change. Such action is unavoidable for it means our very survival spiritually and naturally.

On the Day of Judgment, will God take the excuse of our sins due to another, another group's racism? No, God will ask the Son, "Is this person's name in the book?" Jesus will say either yes or no. That individual person will either enter eternal rest or will suffer eternally in hell, excuses or no excuse (Matthew 25:41). This life is serious business and it is the responsibility and call of those shepherds to guide the flock in all soberness to safety in our Savior. Nowhere is it taught that immoral action is allowed by God due to historical perspective, nor are we permitted to yield to moral decline redefined by the world as relativism. We are to hate what God hates, and that is evil. Our days of removing specks from the man's eye must yield to removing the motes of pride, idolatry, hypocrisy, lying and rebellion from our eye. We even need to clear the mirror to get a good look at ourselves. Moreover, we do not have to collectively pray Psalms 26:2 as it is obvious that we haven't even been trying. We must see ourselves as the prodigal son and repent.

The prodigal son type is easy to identify from the annuals of church history. The African was adopted into God's family as the message of Christ spread across the northern continent. The Islamic military conquest of the seventh and eighth centuries swept Christianity from Africa. In the far away lands of idolatry the black prodigal was lost until found through the unsavory machinations of colonialism and slavery. In our ancestors oppressed state the means to return to the Father was presented albeit reluctantly or for other reasons. The path home was through the gospel of Jesus Christ. The path to restoration in the world's eyes began in the 1960s, yet now spiritually we have been stepping backwards out of our Father's house toward the distant country (Luke 15:13b) all the while protesting the elder brother's (Whites) attitude to the Father. While it is not to say that all the protests are illegitimate, but rather the matter of concern is our foot back on the road to perdition.

It is the messenger's hope that the painful message is heeded to save Black Americans from God's righteous judgment and produce a true spirit of submission to our savior, Jesus Christ.

ENDNOTES

Introduction

1. Kinnon, Joy Bennett. "The Shocking State of Black Marriage," *Ebony,* Nov 2003, 192-194.

2. Levin, Gary. "Idol Contestant Booted for Working for Adult Web Site," *USA Today,* 11 Feb 2003.

3. Komarow, Steven, Richard Willing, and Larry Copeland. "Soldier Held in Deadly Grenade Attack on 101st," *USA Today,* 24 Mar 2003, 31 Oct 2003. <http://www.usatoday.com/news/world/iraq/2003-03-22-war-kuwait-attack_x.html>.

4. X, Marvin. "The New Nat Turner: Hasan Akbar," *Davey D's Hip Hop Corner.* 23 Mar, 2003, 31 Oct 2003. <http://www.daveyd.com/commentarynewnatturner.html>.

5. "Trucker Charged as 18 Die in Trailer," *Jefferson City News Tribune,* 15 May, 2003, 24 Oct 2003<http://www.newstribune.com/stories/051503/war_0515030904.asp.html>.

6. Bryan, Bill. "Secrets Died with Serial Killer.*" St. Louis Post-Dispatch,* 8 June 2003, late ed.: news A1.

7. Corbell, Beverly. "Expert: Black Serial Killers not so Uncommon." *The Advertiser,* 22 June 2003. 25 Oct 2003. <http://cgi.newsweaver.net/cgi-bin/linkweaver/print.pl?url=http://www.acadiananow.com/...html>.

8. "Jury Finds Texas Woman Guilty of Murder in Windshield Death of Homeless Man." *North County Times.* 27 June 2003. 24 Oct 2003. <http://www.nctimes.net/news/2003/20030627/60127.html>.

9. Arce, Rose. "Jayson Blair Sells Tell-all book." *CNN.* 10 Sept 2003. 25 Oct 2003. <http:www.cnn.com/2003/SHOWBIZ/books/09/10/jayson.blair.book.html>.

10. "Tot Survives Three Weeks Alone on Mustard, Ketchup, Dried Pasta." *St. Louis Post-Dispatch.* 1 Oct 2003, Nation.

11. "Woman Kills her Mother and Minister at Church." *St. Louis Post-Dispatch.* 6 Oct 2003, Nation.: A5

12. Harden, Clay. "Bond Reduced in Deadly Yazoo Fire*." The Clarion Ledger.* 9 Oct 2003. <http://www.clarionledger.com/news/0310/09/m03.html>.

13. Bryan, Bill. "Eyewitnesses Describe Infant's Horrid beating." *St. Louis Post-Dispatch.* 8 Oct 2003.

14. Barakat, Matthew. "Accused Sniper Fires Lawyers as Trial Starts." *St. Louis Post-Dispatch.* 21 Oct 2003, late ed.:A.

15. Kaufman, Leslie. "Abuse Case Highlights Dangers of Adoption Incentives program." *St. Louis Post-Dispatch.* 29 Oct 2003, early ed.: A5.

16. Bryan, Bill. "Police Arrest 2 in String of Violent Crimes." *St. Louis Post-Dispatch*. 12 Aug 2003, late ed.: A1.

17. Holly, Derrill. "Crime Spike Shakes Up U.S. Capitol." *St. Louis Post-Dispatch*. 24 Aug 2003, NEWS.

18. Statistics compiled by count of denominational membership provided by "Religion." *African American Desk Reference*. New York: New York Public Library, 1999.

19. "New 'Buying Power' Report Shows Blacks Still Outspend Other Ethnic Segments." *Target Market News*. 17 Oct 2003. <http://www.targetmarketnews.com/buying%20report%2003.html>.

20. McWhorter, John. *Losing the Race: Self Sabotage in Black America*. New York: Simon & Schuster, 2001.

CHAPTER 1 – HOW DID WE GET HERE?

1. Fuson, Tobert H. *The Log of Christopher Columbus.* Camden:International Marine, 1987.

2. Gonzalez, Justo. *The Story of Christianity: The Reformation to the Present Day.* Harper Collins: New York, 1985. 219-220.

3. Emerson, Michael O., and Christian Smith. *Divided By Faith: Evangelical Religion and the Problem of Race in America.* New York: Oxford University Press, 2000.

4. Copeland, Larry. "Church and State Standoffs Spread of USA." *USA Today,* 30 Sept 2003. 15A.

5. Fuson, Robert H. *The Log of Christopher Columbus.* Camden: International Marine, 1987. 107.

6. Keener, Craig S. and Glenn Usry. *Defending Black Faith: Answers to Tough Questions about African-*

American Christianity. Downers Grove: InterVarsity Press, 1997.

CHAPTER 2 – NON-CLERICAL PROPHETS

1. "Fresh Air." *National Public Radio,* WHYY, Philadelphia. 10 Sept 2003.

2. Williams, Juan, and Quinton Dixie. *This Far By Faith: Stories from the African American Religious Experience.* New York: Harper Collins, 2003. 297

3. Terkel, Studs. *Will the Circle Be Unbroken: Reflections on Death, Rebirth, and Hunger for a Faith.* New York: The New Press, 2001. 250

4. Wilson, James Q. "Why We Don't Marry." *City Journal* Winter 2002.

5. Herbert, Bob. "Civil Rights, the Sequel." *NYTimes.com* 7 Jul 2003.

<http://www.nytimes.com/2003/07/07/opinion/07HERB.html?

Ex=1058586312&ei=1&en=f8a8fd4363ac966

6. DeLeon, Lauren Adams. "Braveheart." *Emerge* Oct. 1996: 18.

7. "Fresh Air" *National Public Radio*, WHYX Boston 14 Oct 2003.

8. Chappell, Kevin. "Bernie Mac: TV Father Says Stop Coddling Our Children."

Ebony. June 2003.

9. Gates, Henry Louis, Jr. "After The Revolution." *The New Yorker*. 29 April 1996, 6 May 1996: 59.

10. Associated Press Release. *L.A. Daily News*. 7 Feb 2003, 15 Feb 2003.

<http://www.dailynews.com/stories/0,1413,200~26898~116 4282,00.html>

11. Remnick, David. "Dr. Wilson's Neighborhood." *The New Yorker*. 29 April1996,

6 May 1996:96-107.

12. See endnote in introduction.

CHAPTER 3 – MORALITY BY NUMBERS

1. Joiner, Robert. "Playing the Blame Game." Editorial. *St. Louis Post Dispatch*. 20 Oct 2003.

2. United States, *U.S. Bureau of the Census the Black Population in the United States*: March 2002. Washington: GPO, April 2003.

3. "Religion." *The New York Public Library African American Desk Reference. New York:* Stonesong Press 1999. Denomination date was tallied and the sum total subtracted from the total population. The resulting figure represented 81% of the population as opposed to the widely repeated 90% which source was hard to verify. The 81% number is utilized throughout the book. New denomination statistical information was

difficult to come by as many of the major Black denominations fail to have working websites at the time of this writing.

4. "New 'Buying Power' report shows blacks still outspend other ethnic segments." *Target Market News.* 11 Aug 2003, 17 Oct 2003.

http://www.targetmarketnews.com/buying%20Power%20report%2003.html.

5. United States. Central Intelligence Agency. *World Factbook.* Langley: GPO, Oct 2003. <http://www.cia.gov/publications/factbook/geos.html> 30 Oct 2003.

6. United States. *U.S. Bureau of the Census Poverty in the United States*: 1995. Washington: GPO 1993, 60-194, also John McWhorter. *Losing the Race: Self-Sabotage in Black America.* New York Harper Collins 2000.

7. United States. U.S. Department of Health and Human Services Administration for Children & Families.

Abandoned Babies – Preliminary National Estimates. Washington: GPO.

8. United States. U.S. Bureau of the Census. *Children's Living Arrangements and Characteristics*: March 2002. Washington. GPO June 2003. 6 June 2003. http://www.act.hhs.gov/news/stats/abandon.html (17 Oct 2003) U.S. Department of Health and Human Services National Clearinghouse on Child Abuse and Neglect Information.

9. United States. National Adoption Information Clearinghouse. *Foster Care National Statistics.* Washington: GPO June 2003. <http://www.calib.com/nccanch.html> (25 Oct 2003).

10. United States, U.S. Bureau of Census. *Money Income in the United States.* Washington: GPO 2000.

11. United States, U.S. Department of Health and Human Services, Centers for Disease Control & Prevention, National Center for HIV, STD, and TB Prevention.

Surveillance Report – Volume 12, Number 2 Atlanta: 10 Aug 2001.
<http://www.cdc.gov/hiv/stats/hasr1202/table20.html> (30 Aug 2003).

12. United States, U.S. Department of Health and Human Services, Centers for Disease Control & Prevention. *Tracking the Hidden Epidemics*. Trends in STDs in the United States 2000. Washington: GPO 2000.

13. United States, National Gambling Impact Study Commission, Final Report. *"Problem and Pathological Gambling."* Washington: GPO 18 Jun 1999. < h t t p : / w w w . c a s i n o - gambling–reports.com/GamblingStudy/ProblemGam bling/ page10html> (30 Aug 2003).

14. United States, U.S. Department of Education, Office of Special Education Programs.*Twenty-third Annual Report to Congress on the Implementation of the Individuals with Disabilities Education Act.* W a s h i n g t o n :   1 4   M a y   2 0 0 2 .

http://www.ed.gov/offices/OSERS/OSEP/Products/O
SDP2001An1Rpt/ExecSumm.html> (30 Aug 2003)

15. United States. National Center for Juvenile Justice.
Juvenile Offenders and Victims: 1999 *National Report*.
Washington: GPO Sept 1999. pp150, 192-197.

16. United States. Federal Bureau of Prisons. *Federal
Bureau of Prisons: Quick Facts*. Aug 2003
<http://www.bop.gov/fact0598.html> (2 Sept 2003).

17. United States, Centers for Disease Control and
Prevention, National Center for Injury Prevention and
Control, Division of Violence Prevention. Washington:
GPO 20 Mar 1998.

18. United States. U.S. Department of Health and Human
Services, National Institute of Health, National
Institute of Diabetes & Digestive Kidney Diseases.
Washington: GPO July 2003.
<http://niddk.nih.gov/health/nutrit/pubs/statobes.html
> (8 Sept 2003).

19. Morin, Richard. "The Color of Tips." *Washington Post*, 6 June 2003, 7 June 2003. <http://www.washingtonpost.com/wp-dyn/articles/A26773-2003June.html>

20. United States. U.S. Department of Justice, Federal Bureau of Investigation *Uniform Crime Reports*. Crime in the United States 2000. Washington: GPO 2003, pp 236.

21. United States. U.S. Department of Health and Human Services, Substance Abuse and Mental Health Services Administration Office of Applied Studies. *The DASIS Report*. Arlington: 29 Mar 2003.
<http://www.DrugAbuseStatistic.samhsa.gov> (30 Aug 2003)

22. United States. National Institute of Health, National Cancer Institute, *Patterns of Cancer in the United States 1988-1992*. Bethesda: 1996 NIH Pub. No. 96-4104

23. Webb, Gary. "Dark Alliance: The Story Behind the Crack Explosion." *San Jose Mercury News.* 19 Aug 1996.

24. Valentine, Victoria. "The Courage to Publish." *Emerge.* Jan 1997: 36.

25. Nichols, Thomas M. "Putin's First Two Years: Democracy or Authoritarianism?" *Current History.* Oct 2002:310.

26. "Why (some) Women Like Bad Boys." *Ebony.* April 2003. 73-74, 76. It must be noted that Ebony did not site an author for this article.

CHAPTER 4 – MEDIA AND CULTURAL PROPAGANDA

1. Gitlin, Todd. *Media Unlimited.* New York: Metropolitan Books. 2001.

2. Zengotita, Thomas de. "The Numbing of the American Mind: Culture as Aesthetic." *Harpers*. Apr 2002: 35.

3. Pascal, Blaire. *Pascal's Pensees*. Translation by Martin Turnell. London: Harrill Press. 1962.

4. Rutherford, Ward. *Hitler's Propaganda Machine*. London: Bison Books. 1978.

5. "Study Says Rap is Bad for Black Girls." *St. Louis American*. 6-12 Nov 2003, Vol 75 No. 34: A1, A6.

6. Frame, John M. *Contemporary Worship Music: A Biblical Defense*. Phillipsburg: P&R Publishing, 1997, and Daniel Frankforter. Stones for Bread: *A Critique of Contemporary Worship*. Louisville: Westminister John Knox Press, 2001.

7. Gallick, Sarah. *J.Lo: The Secrets Behind Jennifer Lopez's Climb to the Top*. Boca Raton: AMI Books 2003.

8.   Why (some) Women Like Bad Boys." *Ebony.* April 2003. 73-74, 76. It must be   noted that Ebony did not site an author fro this article.

9. Peterson, Deb. "Channel 46's UPN party draws Mo'nique and a Batch of Bakulas." *St. Louis Post Dispatch.* 3 Apr 2003, section D2.

10. "The Blue Tube: Foul Language on Prime Time Network TV." *Parents Television Council State of the Television Industry Report.* 24 Sept 2003, 26 Sept 2003.

   <http://www.parentstv.org/PTC/publications/reports/ stateindustrylanguage/main.as p.html>

11. "African-American Television Usage: Daytime, Primetime, Late Night." *Nielsen Media Research.* 9 Oct 2003.
    <http://www.nielsonmedia.com/ethnicmeasure/africaname rican/A Adaytime.html>
    <http://www.nielsonmedia.com/ethnicmeasure/africaname rican/A Aprimetime.html>

<http://www.nielsonmedia.com/ethnicmeasure/africaname rican/AAlatenight.html>

12. See previous note.

CHAPTER 5 – THE STATE OF THE INDIVIDUAL

1. Lasch, Christopher. *The Culture of Narcissism: American Life in an Age of Diminishing Expectations*. New York: W.W. Norton, 1979.

2. Keyes, Dick. *Beyond Identity: Finding Your Way in the Image and Character of God*. Carlisle Partnership Publishing, 1998.

3. Rassmussen, Larry L. *Dietrich Bonhoeffer: Reality and Resistance*. Nashville: Abingdon Press, 1972.

Chapter 6 - Education

1. Reid, Karla Scoon. "Meager Effort Said to Fuel Racial Gap." *Education Week.* 12 Mar 2003, Volume 22:1, 18.

2. "The Look of Abercrombie & Fitch." *60 Minutes.* KMOV, St. Louis. 7 Dec 2003.

3. Goldsmith, Susan. "Rich, Black, Flunking." 23 May 2003. 9 Oct 2003. <http://freerepublic.com/focus/f-news/916557/post.html>

4. Ravitch, Diane. *The Language Police: How Pressure Groups Resist What Students Learn.* New York: Knopf, 2003.

Chapter 7 – Law and Order

1. Reed, Fred, "Police, Race, and the Fourth Estate: Have Cops Gone on Strike? *Soldier of Fortune Magazine.* Aug, 2001: 48-51.

2. Schlosser, Eric. *Reefer Madness*. Boston: Houghton Mifflin, 2003.

CHAPTER 8 – MARRIAGE AND SEX DEVALUED

1. Rugoff, Milton. *Prudery & Passion*. New York: Putnam, 1971.

2. Manning, Wendy D., and Kathleen A. Lamb. "Adolescent Well-Being in Cohabiting, Married, and Single-Parent Families." *Journal of Marriage and Family* 65 (2003): 876-91.

3. Schlosser, Eric. *Reefer Madness*. Boston: Houghton Mifflin, 2003.

4. Same as above

5. Page, Clarence. "Nelly's new Pimp Juice drink sends a mixed message. *St. Louis Post Dispatch*. 16 Sept 2003.

Nelly's plans to market an energy drink by the same name stirred a murmuring of controversy but did little harm to Nelly's nice guy rapper image. Strident criticism was absent in Nelly's hometown (and the author's). *St. Louis Press.*

6. Rosenbaum, Robert A. "Clinton Impeachment." *The Penguin Encyclopedia of American History.* New York: Penguin Books, 2003.

7. Berlin, Ira and Leslie S. Rowland. *Families and Freedom: A Documentary History of African-American Kinship in the Civil War Era.* New York: The New Press, 2002.

8. Loewen, James W. *Lies Across America: What our Historic Sites Get Wrong.* New York: The New Press, 1999.

9. Mulrine, Anna. "Risky Business." *U.S. News & World Report Magazine*, 2002: 42-49.

10. Buford, Michelle. "Girls and Sex: You Won't Believe What's Going On." *O*. Nov 2002.

11. IBD

12. Nichols, Bill. "Conservatives Cheer Mini-Series Cancellation." *USA Today*. 5 Nov 2003, 6A.

13. Rutgers University. "The State of Our Unions 2003" *The National Marriage Project*. Piscatany: 2003.

14. See above

15. "Americans Describe Their Views About Life After Death." *Barna Research Online*. 21 Oct 2003. <http://www.barna.org/cgi-in/PagePressRelease.asp?PressReleaseID=150&Reference=A.html>

CHAPTER 9 – THE STATE OF BLACK CLERGY

1. Hamilton, Charles V. *The Black Preacher in America.* New York: William Marrow & Co., 1972.

2. "Abortion Statistics." *AbortionTV.com.* 6 Oct 2003. http://www.abortiontv.com/AbortionStatistics.html.

3. "How wider use of a pill could quiet abortion fights." Editorial. *USA Today.* 30 Dec 2003, 12A.

4. Stricherz, Mark. "Abortion has cost 13 million African American lives."

5. Gay marriage, civil rights aren't linked, some blacks say." *St. Louis Post Dispatch,* 30 Nov 2003. three star ed.

6. "Taking It to the Streets." *The Connection WBUR,* National Public Radio, Boston, 2 June 2003.

7. Gere, Richard. "Razzle Dazzle." *Chicago.* Epic Records, 2002.

8. McMickle, Mavin A. *Preaching to the Black Middle Class: Words of Challenge, Words of Hope.* Valley Forge: Judson Press, 2000.

9. Edwards, Jonathan. "Sin and wickedness bring calamity and misery on a people." *Jonathan Edwards Sermons and Discourses* 1723-1729. Ed. Kenneth P. Minkema. New Haven: Yale UP, 1997. 487.

10. Peterson, Robert A. *HELL ON TRIAL: The Case for Eternal Punishment.* Phillipsburg: P&R Publishing., 1995.

11. Terkel, Studs. *Will the Circle Be Unbroken?* New York: New Press, 2001.

12. Fant, Clyde E. *Bonhoeffer: Worldly Preaching.* Nashville: Thomas Nelson, 1975.

13. Peterson, Jesse Lee. *SCAM.* Nashville: WND, 2003.

14. Williams, Juan. *This Far By Faith.* New York: William Marrow, 2003.

15. McGreery, John T. "Culture vs. Faith." *Chicago Tribune*, 30 Nov 2003, late ed.: sec.14.

16. The Howard Stern Show. WXRK, New York, 17 Sept 2003.

17. McWhorter, John. *Losing the Race: Self-Sabotage in Black America.* New York: Simon & Schuster, 2001.

18. Gilligan, James. *Violence: Our Deadly Epidemic and Its Causes.* New York: Putnam, 1996.

19. Briggs, Jimmie. "No Finish Lines." *Emerge.* Jun 1994: 54-57.

20. Walston, Vaughn. "African American Mobilization." *Mission Frontiers.* Apr 2000. 19 Feb 2003. <http://missionfrontiers.org/2000/02/walston.html>.

21. McMickle, Marvin A. *An Encyclopedia of African American Christian Heritage.* Valley Forge: Judson Press, 2002.

22. See above

23. *No More Secrets, No More Lies.* Dir. Slan Hatch. Videocassette. King & King Training, 2002.

CHAPTER 10 – END GAME

1. "Uganda's ABC Program." *All Things Considered.* National Public Radio, Washington, D.C. 1 Jan 2004. Uganda's HIV rate of 30% of the population has been cut to 6%.

2. Hyton, Wil S. "Sick On the Inside." *Harpers.* Aug 2003. 43-54.

3. Williams, Juan. *This Far By Faith.* New York: William Marrow, 2003. 290.

4. "Tearing Down Cabrin: Green." Prod. Michael Bronner. *60 Minutes.* New York. 23 July 2003.

Rodrick Burton

Appendix A

RESOLUTION ON RACIAL RECONCILIATION ON THE 150TH ANNIVERSARY OF THE SOUTHERN BAPTIST CONVENTION
June 1995

WHEREAS, Since its founding in 1845, the Southern Baptist Convention has been an effective instrument of God in missions, evangelism, and social ministry; and

WHEREAS, The Scriptures teach that Eve is the mother of all living (Genesis 3:20), and that God shows no partiality, but in every nation whoever fears him and works righteousness is accepted by him (Acts 10:34-35), and that God has made from one blood every nation of men to dwell on the face of the earth (Acts 17:26); and

WHEREAS, Our relationship to African-Americans has been hindered from the beginning by the role that slavery played in the formation of the Southern Baptist Convention; and

WHEREAS, Many of our Southern Baptist forbears defended the right to own slaves, and either participated in, supported, or acquiesced in the particularly inhumane nature of American slavery; and

WHEREAS, In later years Southern Baptists failed, in many cases, to support, and in some cases opposed, legitimate initiatives to secure the civil rights of African-Americans; and

WHEREAS, Racism has led to discrimination, oppression, injustice, and violence, both in the Civil War and throughout the history of our nation; and

WHEREAS, Racism has divided the body of Christ and Southern Baptists in particular, and separated us from our African-American brothers and sisters; and

WHEREAS, Many of our congregations have intentionally and/or unintentionally excluded African-Americans from worship, membership, and leadership; and

WHEREAS, Racism profoundly distorts our understanding of Christian morality, leading some Southern Baptists to believe that racial prejudice and discrimination are compatible with the Gospel; and

WHEREAS, Jesus performed the ministry of reconciliation to restore sinners to a right relationship with the Heavenly Father, and to establish right relations among all human beings, especially within the family of faith.

Therefore, be it RESOLVED, That we, the messengers to the Sesquicentennial meeting of the Southern Baptist Convention, assembled in Atlanta, Georgia, June 20-22, 1995, unwaveringly denounce racism, in all its forms, as deplorable sin; and

Be it further RESOLVED, That we affirm the Bibles teaching that every human life is sacred, and is of equal and immeasurable worth, made in Gods image, regardless of race or ethnicity (Genesis 1:27), and that, with respect to salvation through Christ, there is neither Jew nor Greek, there is neither slave nor free, there is neither male nor female, for (we) are all one in Christ Jesus (Galatians 3:28); and

Be it further RESOLVED, That we lament and repudiate historic acts of evil such as slavery from which we continue to reap a bitter harvest, and we recognize that the racism which yet plagues our culture today is inextricably tied to the past; and

Be it further RESOLVED, That we apologize to all African-Americans for condoning and/or perpetuating individual and systemic racism in our lifetime; and we genuinely repent of racism of which we have been guilty, whether consciously (Psalm 19:13) or unconsciously (Leviticus 4:27); and

Be it further RESOLVED, That we ask forgiveness from our African-American brothers and sisters, acknowledging that our own healing is at stake; and

Be it further RESOLVED, That we hereby commit ourselves to eradicate racism in all its forms from Southern Baptist life and ministry; and

Be it further RESOLVED, That we commit ourselves to be doers of the Word (James 1:22) by pursuing racial reconciliation in all our relationships, especially with our brothers and sisters in Christ (1 John 2:6), to the end that our light would so shine before others, that they may see (our) good works and glorify (our) Father in heaven (Matthew 5:16); and

Be it finally RESOLVED, That we pledge our commitment to the Great Commission task of making disciples of all people (Matthew 28:19), confessing that in the church God is calling together one people from every tribe and nation (Revelation 5:9), and proclaiming that the Gospel of our Lord Jesus Christ is the only certain and sufficient ground upon which redeemed persons will stand together in restored family union as joint-heirs with Christ (Romans 8:17).

Atlanta, Georgia

http://www.sbc.net/resolutions/amResolution.asp?ID=899

Appendix B

MINUTES OF THE GENERAL ASSEMBLY

30TH General Assembly, 2002

During the annual meeting of the General Assembly of the Presbyterian Church in America that met in Birmingham in mid-June, the following resolution was overwhelmingly embraced with a standing ovation.

Whereas the heinous sins attendant with unbiblical forms of servitude-- including oppression, racism, exploitation, manstealing, and chattel slavery-- stand in opposition to the Gospel," and,

Whereas the effects of these sins have created and continue to create barriers between brothers and sisters of different races and/or economic spheres,' and, Whereas the aftereffects of these sins continue to be felt

197

in the economic, cultural, and social affairs of the communities in which we live and minister.

We, therefore, confess our involvement in these sins. As a people, both we and our fathers have failed to keep the commandments, the statutes, and the laws God has commanded.

We, therefore, publicly repent of our pride, our complacency, and our complicity. Furthermore, we seek the forgiveness of our brothers and sisters for the reticence of our hearts that have constrained us from acting swiftly in this matter.

OVERTURE 14 from Rocky Mountain Presbytery (to CCB & B & O *"Amend BCO* 24-1 to Replace "should" With "shall"

Whereas the *BCO* 24-1, line 5, states that a "...prospective officer should be an active male member. . ." using subjunctive mood to indicate a likely rather expected case; and

Whereas the normal circumstance for prospective officers must be an active and committed male member in a local PCA congregation; and

Whereas the indicative mood "shall" would better express the norm for prospective candidates;

Therefore the Rocky Mountain Presbytery, meeting April 26, 2001, respectfully overtures the   General Assembly to replace the word "should" in line 5 of *BCD* 24-1 with the word "shall".

The new reading would then be "... keeping in mind each prospective officer shall be an active male member..."

That Overture 15 from Rocky Mountain Presbytery ("Amend *BCO* 24-1 to Specify "men" Rather Than "persons" be answered in the negative. [See also 30-29, III, p. 101.]

Adopted

Grounds: In this context "persons" refers to men. *BCO 7-2* states "... these offices are open to men only." BCO 24-1 provides, "...keeping in mind that prospective officer should be an active male member meets the qualifications set forth in I Timothy 3 and Titus 1." It is worth noting that the term in question has been in this place since the original constitution of the PCUSA in 1788, so there can be no suggestion of unwholesome contemporary influence in its employment.

OVERTURE 15 from Rocky Mountain Presbytery (to CCB & B & O "Amend *BCO* 24-1 to Specify "men" Rather Than "persons'

Whereas, the Bible makes clear that the office of elder is for men only (see I Tim 2:12, I Tim 3:2 and Titus 1:6 [husband of one wife]) and

Whereas, the PCA has consistently and unashamedly held this view and

Whereas, while there may be some Biblical and exegetical disagreement about the ordination of women to the office of deacon among some in the PCA; yet at present the office of deacon is also available only to men (see I Timothy 3:2 [husband of one wife]) and

Whereas, the *BCO* 24-1, line one, says "persons" which is gender neutral rather than men;

Therefore Rocky Mountain Presbytery, meeting on April 26, 2001, respectfully overtures the General Assembly to replace the word "persons" in line one of BCQ 24-.1, with word "men".

The new reading would then be "Every church shall elect men to the offices of ruling elder and deacon ..."

That the General Assembly refer Overture 19 from Chesapeake Presbytery ("Erect a Study Committee on Ministry Amidst Ethnic Diversity") to the Committee of Commissioners on Mission to North America for their recommendation to the General Assembly.
[For text and action, see 30-31, Ill; 18, p. 188.]

That the General Assembly pause for prayer before beginning consideration *of* Overture 20, [see text and action at 30-53, III, 14, p. 262] and that the General Assembly suspend RAO 17- 4.d to allow 30 minutes on the main motion, without a motion for the previous question being in order, after the Committee, through its appointed representatives, has the opportunity to speak in favor *of* the Committee's recommendation for 10 minutes.

Adopted in *accordance with RAQ* 1.8

That Overture 20 from Nashville Presbytery ("Racial Reconciliation") be answered by the adoption of the following statement.

Adopted

Whereas, the heinous sins attendant with unbiblical forms of servitude-including oppression, racism, exploitation, manstealing, and chattel slavery-stand in to the Gospel; and,

Whereas, the effects of these sins have created and continue to create barriers between brothers and sisters of different races and/or economic spheres; and

Whereas, the aftereffects of these sins continue to be felt in the economic, cultural, and social affairs of communities in which we live and minister;

We therefore confess our involvement in these sins. As a people, both we and our fathers have failed to keep the commandments, the statutes, and the laws God has commanded. We therefore publicly repent of our pride, our complacency, and our complicity. Furthermore, we seek the forgiveness of our brothers and sisters for the reticence of our hearts that have constrained us from acting swiftly in this matter.

We will strive, in a manner consistent with the Gospel imperatives, for the encouragement of racial reconciliation, the establishment of urban and minority congregations, and the enhancement of existing ministries of mercy in our cities, among the poor, and across all social, racial, and economic boundaries, to the glory of God. Amen.

Note:

The Presbyterian Church in America participated in addressing the question of racial reconciliation as early as 1977, through her delegation to the NAPARC conference on race relations, and the resulting statement adopted.

That statement achieved a "consensus on a number of crucial issues" and it began by confessing serious inadequacies with respect to NAPARC member churches concerning race relations in the church:

We are convinced that we, as Reformed Christians, have failed to speak and act boldly in the area of race relations. Our denominational profiles reveal patterns of ethnic and racial homogeneity. We believe that this situation fails to give adequate expression to the saying purposes *of* our sovereign God, whose covenant extends to all peoples and races. "

We are convinced that our record in this crucial area is one of racial brokenness and disobedience. In such a situation the credibility of our Reformed witness, piety and doctrinal confession is at stake. We have not lived out the implications of that biblical and confessional heritage which we hold in common with each other, with its emphasis on the sovereignty and freedom of grace, on the absence of human merit in gaining salvation, and on the responsibility to subject all of life to the Lordship of Christ.

The statement continued with a summary of faithful biblical teaching adapted to address the defects confessed above:

> Although there are marked distinctions and even divisions among men, including those of race, mankind, according to the teaching of the Bible, has a single origin. Later distinctions and divisions are indeed significant and may not simply be pushed aside; nevertheless, the Bible clearly teaches that the gospel is universal in its offer and its call. All men are created in the image of God and have fallen into sin, and are in need of redemption. All those who are in Christ are united together with Him as their Head in a new humanity, in which the distinctions and divisions that otherwise separate men are transcended in a new unity. True, the distinctions mentioned in the Bible as

having been overcome in Christ are not primarily those of race, nor does the Bible think along lines that correspond with the distinctions of race as we understand them today; nevertheless, racial distinctions and divisions as we know and understand them today certainly fall under those things that have been transcended in Christ. How, then, is the new unity in Christ to be expressed in the communion of the church today as it bears on the question of race?

The description of God's people in I Peter 2:9, 10, as a chosen generation, a royal priesthood, a holy nation, reveals the church's visible oneness as the community of those separated into the Lord. It is a oneness on the order of the racial, cultic, and national unity of Israel (Exodus 19:6), and it has the wonderful works of God. Therefore, the church's identity transcends and makes of secondary importance the racial, national and cultic identities of the world.

We see in Revelation 7:9, 10, the chosen race worshiping the Lamb in heaven. They come from different backgrounds, yet worship with one voice. Is-not the unity of our worship here on earth to be a copy of that which takes place within the heavenly sanctuary? Should not all those washed in the blood of the Lamb joyously worship together?

In the light of such scriptural teaching, the continued in the acknowledgement of sin on the part member churches:

> In repentance we acknowledge and confess that we have failed effectively to recognize the full humanity of other races and the similarity of their needs, desires, and hopes to ours; and thus we have failed to love our neighbor as ourselves. . . Within the church, our members have exhibited such attitudes and actions as discourage membership or participation by minority groups...Our churches have not been free from such formal actions as discourage membership or participation by minority groups. They have been guilty of a lack of positive action concerning mission to ethnic groups in their neighborhoods and to ethnic groups at large. They have practiced a kind of cultural exclusivism, thinking of the church as "our church" rather than Christ's involves the sins of pride and idolatry.

Yet the statement was able to acknowledge the work of grace evident in this matter, particularly in the seminaries that serve the PCA:

We commend... Westminster Theological Seminary for its ministerial institute, which intends to assist inner-city pastors in their continued training in ministry and Covenant Theological Seminary for its Urban Ministers' Institute...

The statement concluded with a number of exhortations, among which are included:

We encourage congregations to reach out to the entire community around them. We encourage congregations to rise to meet the challenge of racial diversity in changing neighborhoods.

We encourage members of our congregations to remain in those communities were there are racially changing patterns.

We acknowledge that in order to change our unbiblical profile, we should urge churches in NAPARC to give priority to a vigorous pursuit of evangelism and church planting in racially, economically, and ethnically diverse communities. . ..

In reaffirming the great commission, we recommend . . . that cross-cultural evangelism be encouraged in our churches through preaching, modeling, and disciplining, through the elders and pastors, beginning with the use of our covenant families and homes, and house-to-house neighborhood outreach.

OVERTURE 20 from Nashville Presbytery (to B&O) "Racial Reconciliation"

Whereas, the Scriptures portray a covenantal pattern of both celebration of our rich heritage and repentance for the sins of our fathers; and,

Whereas, our nation has been blessed even as we have repeatedly addressed iniquity, redressed injustice, and assessed restitution for our inconsistent application of the ideals of truth and freedom; and,

Whereas, the heinous sins attendant with unbiblical forms of servitude-including oppression, racism, exploitation, manstealing, and chattel slavery-remain among the defining features of our national history; and,

Whereas, the issues surrounding that part of our history continue to shape our national life, even creating barriers between brothers and sisters of different races and/or economic spheres from enjoying: unencumbered Christian fellowship with one another and,

Whereas, the aftereffects of that part of our history continue to be felt in the economic, cultural, and social affairs of the communities in which we live and minister.

We therefore confess our covenantal involvement in national sins. As a people, both we and our fathers have failed to keep the commandments, the statutes, and the laws our God has commanded. We; therefore publicly repent of our pride, our complacency, and our complicity. Furthermore, we seek the forgiveness of our brothers and sisters for the reticence of our hearts, which has constrained us from acting swiftly in this matter.

As a people, we pledge to work hard, in a manner consistent with the Gospel imperatives, for the encouragement of racial reconciliation, the establishment of urban and minority congregations, and the enhancement of existing ministries of mercy in our cities, among the poor, and across all social, racial, and economic boundaries, to the glory of God. Amen.

That Personal Resolution 6 be answered by reference to the Assembly's action with regard to Overture 20. [See 30-53, III, 14, p. 261.]

Whereas, the Presbyterian Church in America was formed to preach and teach the truth of God's Word with the desire that its members would practice and live by the truth and as we are a young denomination meeting together for our 30th Annual General Assembly, we want to thank God for the enabling grace to do this as well as we have done it and confess that when and where we have failed it is our fault and because of our sin; and

Whereas, we acknowledge that corporately as a denomination and individually as members of the Presbyterian Church in America we have sinned, (Romans 3:23)

Whereas, we acknowle that along with our many other sins, we may have corporately or individually sinned by slighting or offending a brother in Christ, and we as the people of God are called on in

Scripture to repent of our sins as God reveals them to us by His Holy Spirit (Rev. 3:19, Acts 16:19-20, Luke 5:32, & II Cor. 7:10); and

Whereas, we recognize that each one of us must repent for our own sins as God holds each of us accountable for them (Ezekiel18:20, Romans 14:12, Jeremiah 31:29- 30, Deuteronomy 24:16), and

Whereas, we also recognize that Scripture establishes precedents for the confession of the past sins of others   without assessing personal responsibility for those past sins to the confessing party (Neh. 1:5-7, Neh. 9:1- 3, Daniel 9:4-19), and

Whereas, we recognize the dangers of sins of omission as being grave as those of the sins of commission (James 4:17, Psalm 51:16-17, Proverbs 21:3, Luke 12:47), and

Whereas, God's Word warns strongly against mistreating or not loving a Christian brother (I Corinthians 6:8, I Thessalonians 4:6, James 4:11-12), and

Whereas, we recognize that some have in the past, by commission and/or by omission, offended and slighted their brothers and sisters in Christ (I John 1:8-10), and

Whereas, we desire that all members of the Presbyterian Church in America conduct themselves first as the people of God - without favoritism, prejudice or partiality (Leviticus 19:15 & I Timothy 5:21), and

Whereas, we desire that all members of the Presbyterian Church in America not only show love for their brothers but that they actually have love for their brothers in their hearts (I John 4:21, Hebrews 13:1, Psalm 133:1 & John 13:34-35)

Appendix C

by Race, 2000—Continued
[9,017 agencies; 2000 estimated population 182,090,101]

Offense charged	Arrests 18 and over					Percent distribution[1]			
	Total	White	Black	American Indian or Alaskan Native	Asian or Pacific Islander	Total	White	Black	Americ Indian Alask Nativ
TOTAL	7,514,175	5,203,623	2,138,492	93,311	78,749	100.0	69.3	28.5	1.2
Murder and nonnegligent manslaughter	7,882	3,854	3,839	83	106	100.0	48.9	48.7	1.1
Forcible rape	14,931	9,534	5,053	173	171	100.0	63.9	33.8	1.2
Robbery	53,887	24,353	28,649	321	564	100.0	45.2	53.2	0.6
Aggravated assault	271,953	173,976	91,487	3,089	3,401	100.0	64.0	33.6	1.1
Burglary	126,333	85,567	38,239	1,138	1,389	100.0	67.7	30.3	0.9
Larceny-theft	536,288	349,285	173,078	6,437	7,488	100.0	65.1	32.3	1.2
Motor vehicle theft	64,596	35,832	26,958	666	1,140	100.0	55.5	41.7	1.0
Arson	5,021	3,659	1,272	45	45	100.0	72.9	25.3	0.9
Violent crime[2]	348,653	211,717	129,028	3,666	4,242	100.0	60.7	37.0	1.1
Property crime[3]	732,238	474,343	239,547	8,286	10,062	100.0	64.8	32.7	1.1
Crime Index total[4]	1,080,891	686,060	368,575	11,952	14,304	100.0	63.5	34.1	1.1
Other assaults	701,050	464,354	219,209	9,915	7,572	100.0	66.2	31.3	1.4
Forgery and counterfeiting	66,628	44,955	20,389	396	888	100.0	67.5	30.6	0.6
Fraud	205,372	138,490	64,430	1,119	1,333	100.0	67.4	31.4	0.5
Embezzlement	11,243	7,172	3,831	49	191	100.0	63.8	34.1	0.4
Stolen property; buying, receiving, possessing	60,104	35,210	23,864	415	615	100.0	58.6	39.7	0.7
Vandalism	109,381	78,635	27,979	1,687	1,080	100.0	71.9	25.6	1.5
Weapons; carrying, possessing, etc.	80,194	47,782	31,010	578	824	100.0	59.6	38.7	0.7
Prostitution and commercialized vice	60,424	35,037	23,859	498	1,030	100.0	58.0	39.5	0.8
Sex offenses (except forcible rape and prostitution)	49,617	37,289	11,107	577	644	100.0	75.2	22.4	1.2
Drug abuse violations	904,886	573,288	320,895	4,561	6,142	100.0	63.4	35.5	0.5
Gambling	6,142	2,077	3,737	26	302	100.0	33.8	60.8	0.4
Offenses against the family and children	84,727	56,737	25,664	885	1,441	100.0	67.0	30.3	1.0
Driving under the influence	887,191	781,720	85,591	11,666	8,214	100.0	88.1	9.6	1.3
Liquor laws	332,398	278,144	41,492	10,266	2,496	100.0	83.7	12.5	3.1
Drunkenness	407,488	344,177	56,734	4,547	2,030	100.0	84.5	13.9	1.1
Disorderly conduct	310,382	202,077	101,232	5,072	2,001	100.0	65.1	32.6	1.6
Vagrancy	19,934	10,270	9,017	550	97	100.0	51.5	45.2	2.8
All other offenses (except traffic)	2,133,229	1,378,180	698,988	28,544	27,517	100.0	64.6	32.8	1.3
Suspicion	2,894	1,969	889	8	28	100.0	68.0	30.7	0.3
Curfew and loitering law violations	...	...	—	—	...	...	...	...	—
Runaways	...	...	—	—	...	...	...	...	...

[1] Because of rounding, the percentages may not add to total.

[2] Violent crimes are offenses of murder, forcible rape, robbery, and aggravated assault.

[3] Property crimes are offenses of burglary, larceny-theft, motor vehicle theft, and arson.

[4] Includes arson.

Appendix D

FSI Lecture Series

What Movies say about Race in America

by Rodrick Burton

INTRODUCTION

One does not need a theological degree to learn that nowhere in the New Testament are Christians called either to condone or practice inequality among believers. Furthermore, scripture text found in James 2: 1-9 clearly prohibits discriminatory actions within in the church. The Apostle Paul repeatedly and explicitly explained that God's new people are united in faith by the sacred blood and atonement of the cross. Sadly, this has not deterred Satan's plans of constructing and maintaining divisive racial and economic inequity regimes inside the Christian community. This is American Christianity's legacy of shame. Mounds of empirical data compiled over the years have conclusively demonstrated the obvious: that the United States is a highly racialized society despite the often celebrated and loudly heralded preeminence of Christianity.

Omar Bradley stated in 1948, "we have grasped the mystery of the atom but rejected the sermon on the mount[1]." Throughout Dr. Emerson's lecture at Covenant it was stressed that white Evangelical Christendom uses three methods to keep the head collectively buried in the sand on the race division issue. They involve a minimizing of the problem; assigning blame to individuals (a few bad apples); and shifting the blame to Blacks. Conversely, if one were to hearken to the rhetoric of prominent Christians they would be led to believe that this country stands as a testament to the faith evidenced by undisputed material blessing. Within this arrogant construct of comfort and unexamined privilege, Christ's unifying message of reconciliation is denied and new stones form for the nonbeliever to hurl accurately. God's justice enabled the Civil Rights Movement to be successful. White Evangelical silence and overt opposition to Blacks' fight for equality under

216

secular law drove scores to view Christianity as an impotent force to change the human condition and question its claims of legitimacy. This occurred at a critical juncture in human history by which modernity transformed into postmodernism. As the youth of the sixties rebelled against the establishment, they turned from the God of their fathers, embracing the old eastern gods, Mohammad's message, and good old-fashioned hedonism.

The aforementioned state represents a dual tragedy. On the one hand, White American Christians have not participated in the truth and reconciliation necessary to restore and build solid bridges across the racial divide. Yet on the other side of the pew, Black Americans have not relinquished the roots of bitterness tied to the holistic forgiveness message Christ taught. The fumbling of the ball by the Christian majority in the 1960s has served as a siege ramp for Lucifer's campaign to promote Christian irrelevancy in the Western world.

Tragically, the continuation of unchallenged or single-sided challenges to eliminate the canyon dividing believers endures. I intend to explore the effects of racialization that Dr. Emerson discussed within the context of film. Finally, I will conclude with a review of Spike Lee's "Clockers" and its relevance to the topic.

CHAPTER 1

HOORAY FOR HOLLYWOOD?

Movies. What are they? What do they mean to us? How ingrained are they in American culture? This is what Roger Ebert had to say about movies:

> We live in a box of space and time. Movies are windows in its walls. They allow us to enter others' minds-not simply in the sense of identifying with the characters, although that is an important part of it, but by seeing the world as another sees it![2]

So from Ebert we glean that movies are an art form that allows others to live through the character's eyes. This art form is unique as the viewer is subject to not only the motion within the picture, but also sound. Seeing a movie is the only way to feel its full impact.

Movies are not just an art, but also a business. Rutgers film professor, John Belton, accurately described the

219

American film industry as an "institution."[3] This institution has always been honest with its proclamations that Hollywood was in the myth making business. Therefore, to sell tickets, Tinseltown's survival instinct is to put the best, most beautiful and idealized face forward. As a consequence, the subject of race relations has been deliberately ignored and romanticized causing American history to be routinely rewritten.

Proverbs 12:17 instructs that a truthful witness gives honest testimony, but a false witness tells lies. As bearers of the ultimate truth, why are Christians silent as fiction is being served up as hot steaming truth. Hollywood's immoral images have been routinely attacked, but its web of historical lies has never been swept clean. The propaganda started in earnest with "Birth of a Nation."

CHAPTER 2

BLACK FILM: CONTEXT AND PERSPECTIVE

Race history affected all comers of American culture, including film history. Regarding that history, it is my contention that from its beginnings the ingrained racialized worldview has been infused into this powerful medium, and has largely served to reinforce racist stereotypes and minimize race problems on through to the present day.

Film critic Nelson George described Black film today as, "been flattened into formulas as a genre better understood as a market niche than an artistic aesthetic."[4] How this came about over the years could be best understood by returning to the early days of film.

During the waking years of American film history in the period of silent movies, a racial bombshell was unleashed called "Birth of a Nation." D. W. Griffith's artful propaganda piece was released to a country caught in the passionate throws of love with a new, revolutionarily medium. Griffin

Rodrick Burton

rewrote southern Reconstruction history by painting the Confederate rebellion as an honorable cause, forever typecasting the Southern society in a manner repeated this very day in films such as "Gods and Generals." The "peculiar institution of slavery" was justified as Griffith depicted the newly empowered freed slaves engaged in corrupt governance and in league with carpetbaggers. The most outrageous assertion made by the film was that Ku Klux Klan's chivalrous origins were in response to free Blacks' designs to sully White-womanhood.[5] This film was a pop culture hit. It was received with such enthusiasm in the south resulting in an immediate spike in the ongoing tragedy that was lynching. President Woodrow Wilson zealously expressed his approval for the film at a time when a racial hierarchy was enforced by Jim Crow laws. After enduring the South's backlash, American Blacks must suffer a national "blame the victim" epidemic brought on by Griffith's visual heresy. The new medium wielded a power and influence that would later be exploited further by the Nazi regime.

Hollywood kept apace with society with its relegation of subservient roles for Blacks. In 1939 the landmark film classic "Gone with the Wind" was released. Yet again another sympathetic Civil War South was the subject. For the first

222

time a Black actress, Hattie McDaniel won an Oscar award for her role as Scarlet O'Hara's personal slave. As time passed, Hollywood churned out cheap productions specifically marketed to Black audiences. President Truman's integration of the armed forces and the need to counter Cold War Communist propaganda spurred Hollywood to sally further into the race relation realm, albeit with great trepidation.

Over the years a small cadre of Black actors and actresses worked in non-racially threatening roles to satisfy White audiences, White actors and directors, with a few notable exceptions *(Guess Who's Coming to Dinner, No Way Out)*. Late Modernism and the revolutionary days of the 1960s seemed to signal an opportunity for more engaging film-making to compliment the changing times. Many blacks found a groundswell of new roles in movies and in television. The problem was television was free and therefore played it safe by sticking to entertainment. Therefore, Black roles were ancillary in nature. As for the road to Tinseltown, it detoured into the Black Exploitation film period. Roles were made abundant to those willing to play pimps, prostitutes, crooks and various antisocial characters. Even famous stars such as Sidney Poitier and Bill Cosby had to do their stint in Panavision and Technicolor filmed stereotyped cesspools. The imagery of the angry, oversexed, criminal-minded Negro served to justify social and religious balkanization.

From the 1970s onward, Hollywood has pressed forward offering escapism, nihilism, and idealized love. Although the ranks of Black actors and actresses have swelled, there exists a handful of Black directors. It was not until 1991 that one was honored for his work. The film academy bestowed its coveted award upon a young adult black director named John Singleton. His urban drama, "The Boys in the Hood," provided a glimpse of the lives of those living in crime plagued South-Central Los Angeles. In the final scene, the character "Dough Boy," played by rapper Ice Kube, utters a statement bemoaning America's indifference to the internecine culling taking place in the urban centers nationwide. Unfortunately, he was wrong. Those living the American dream in suburban settings do care about inner-city violence: they care for it to remain where it is. Again, a critically acclaimed motion picture about Black life reinforced the premise that we need to stay separated from them. The White viewer was able to safely watch in his own home on cable video or even from an advertising trailer yet another movie telling them that Blacks are violent, oversexed, unemployable, and uncivilized. The credibility level was raised due to the fact that a Black man directed it.

As the 20th century passed away, and corporations and Hollywood honed their marketing techniques to target products like smart bombs specifically to certain markets. The costly blockbuster films are tailored to appeal to all audiences, tending to stick to formulas, and avoid the race topic or other substantive issues. This holds true even for the popular independent film market. As in the real-world, the fictional world presents a divided nation as a given.

When one considers the recent historic Academy awards to Halle Berry and Denzel Washington, it is clear the wheel has turned a full circle. This victory must briefly be explored. In 2002 after 74 years and a paltry six prior awards, the American Film Academy issued its first award to a Black woman for best actress (Halle Berry) and simultaneously awarded Denzel Washington for best actor in the same night. A historical night declared by all, especially the industry and Blacks long craving recognition in that field. What happened however, was a historical rerun. Denzel Washington's award winning role was for playing a servant, a civil servant. He played the role of a vile, wicked, morally-depraved narcotics cop who was training a young new detective (Ethan Hawke). Over the course of the "training day," Washington's character tries thoroughly to corrupt this young ,idealistic, upstanding white officer. As the final confrontation plays out in a Black neighborhood so lawless that Washington warns Hawke never to go alone, the hood rejects Washington's authority and honors Hawke's.

Halle Berry plays the role of a servant as well: a sexual servant. In "Monster's Ball" she has a love affair with the son of a racist. So some sixty years after receiving the first Oscars for playing the servant, the new awards again go to Blacks playing the servant.

CHAPTER 4

CLOCKERS: A SERMON ON THE MOUNT

Now I will discuss Spike Lee's most profound and poignant work. *Clockers*, released in 1995, was a story about the inner city drug trade. The film was a joint effort by Lee and Martin Scorsese to bring Richard Price's novel (of the same name) to the screen. Spike Lee received good reviews for his work, but the commentary from the Black community was noticeably muted. The reason being is that the message rang too close to home. Drugs have long plagued the Black community, but never to the degree that was epidemic until the 1960s. While the conspiracy theorists have claimed the government permitted the problem, more than likely the reasons for the initial deluges of heroin relate to Baby-Boom aged Mafioso discarding old guard prohibitions against narcotic sales. Whatever the reason for the heinous epidemic, enterprising disenfranchised Blacks expanded the trade until the neighborhood drug pusher has reached institutional status.

The Crack epidemic and street gang proliferation of the late 1980s spewed forth new waves of urban bloodletting unseen since prohibition days. Spike Lee's *Clockers* peered in on the life of the dealers and the corrosive ripple effects of the trade within and without the Black community.

The main character, Strike (Mekhi Phifer), is a street dealer who comes under suspicion for a murder that his brother has confessed. This older brother (Victor Isaiah Washington) is an upstanding, hard-working family man whose job at a neighborhood restaurant brings him face to face with customers who are also local criminals. One homicide detective, Rocco Klein (Harvey Keitel), resists the cynicism and racism expressed by his partner and digs deeper into a would-be open and shut case. Through Lee's storytelling, the viewer peers at the characters beyond the criminal activity to view secondary communal effects. In the housing projects where the story takes place, the viewers are allowed to witness how people struggle to live and raise children in areas most Americans would consider hell. As so many Black children are born and raised by single parents (seven in ten[6] young men such as Strike reach out to the representing father figures) and so often in crime-plagued areas, this figure is an influential/older criminal. This dynamic is evidenced by some of the scenes between Strike and his boss Rodney Little (Delroy Lindo).

The mask of compassion is ripped away when Little, suspicious of continued police questioning, threatens Strike with death if he ever implicates his employer. Strike replicates this mentoring dynamic by taking a young studious neighborhood kid under his wing and warning him of the street's dangers. Strike's brother, in jail awaiting trial, expects him to raise bail to release him from an environment that so many Black men have grown accustomed to.

The final act reveals the lamentable: those who were working to escape the ghetto become criminal perpetrators and those surviving as predators within the environment continue to ply their vile trade. It is difficult to continue with this review without choking up on the horrible tragedy of it all. Two communities touting a universal faith infused with power from on high have accepted violent ghetto life to be a given. The White Christians for reasons of continued arrogance and benign neglect--and the Black Christians for equally absurd issues involving pride and neglect. The failure of the two to bridge the racial divide tarnishes Christ's message and robs those who would witness the Holy Spirit's power bind two groups together in Christ to uplift the downtrodden and bring life to bastions of death.

CHAPTER 5

THE SUM OF ALL FEARS

As I had previously asserted, the 1960s presented an opportunity for reconciliation as well as an attack pad from which a unified Christian America could've challenged Hollywood's worldview. What remains today are Black films that embody age old stereotypes in new costumes, and these images are left unchallenged by the Black church. Are we so appreciative of acting jobs that we ignore Paul's call to hate what is evil (Romans 12:9)? Are we so pleased to see ourselves on the silver screen we never protest the content? To the White Christians I ask, if it is a worthy cause to unite against abortion, then why is it called Communism when the questions arise about ending poverty or redistributing wealth? Has the worship of American individualism trumped the New Testament calls to unite obediently and serve the faith community? How long will the Black Clergy rally to every public affront, real or perceived?

Christ said that we are to love our neighbor as ourselves, and called this the second most important commandment. To bridge the chasm that continues to divide us we must consider, as did the Jews after hearing Jesus' Samaritan parable, do we know who our neighbors are? Do we love ourselves? Does the world hate us for espousing the faith and failing to live it at home but determined to impose our way of life on others?

I have neighbors that I have known for years. Now I would never sit idly by while one neighbor's basement would disgorge smoke, nor would let another's home to be defaced by vandals without challenging them. Black Christians need help to put the fires out in the cities and White Christians need to lead the charge in challenging Hollywood's divisive lies. I pray for the day this mote in the eye of American Christianity will be removed. I know that sin and the fallen condition of the world will increase until the Messiah's return. However, through him we have access to the power to witness with a unity unknown to these shores. United by faith we could move the mountain into the chasm that divides us.

WHAT MOVIES SAY ABOUT RACE IN AMERICA
ENDNOTES

1   Knowles, Elizabeth, ed. *The Oxford Dictionary of 20th Century-Quotations.* New York: Oxford UP, 1998

2   Ebert, Roger. *The Great Movies.* New York: Broadway Books, 2002

3   Belton, John. *American Cinema/American Culture.* New York: McGraw Hill, 1994.

4   George, Nelson. *Blackface: Reflections on African Americans and the movies.* New York: Coopersquare Press, 2002.

5   Lang, Robert, ed. *The Birth of a Nation.* New Brunswick: Rutgers UP, 1994.

6   United States. *Census 2000.* Washington: 2000.

Rodrick Burton is available for personal appearances and/or speaking engagements.

For more information go to his website at rodrickburton.com or send an email to Rodrick at: rkburton@rodrickburton.com

Rodrick Burton

PO Box 862

Chesterfield, MO 63006-0862

To order additional copies of this or other books call our toll free ordering line: 1-888-383-3110 or visit our online bookstore at www.advantagebookstore.com

Advantage BOOKS

Longwood, Florida, USA

"we bring dreams to life"™
www.advbooks.com

4

Printed in the United States
26352LVS00006B/115-117